10 RULES FOR

RESILIENCE

MENTAL TOUGHNESS FOR FAMILIES

10 RULES FOR

RESILIENCE

JOE DE SENA

with Dr. Lara Pence

HarperOne
An Imprint of HarperCollinsPublishers

Page 100: Quotation from Richard Branson from *Spartan Up!* podcast, episode 25, March 9, 2015.

HarperCollins books may be purchased for educational, business, or sales promotional use. For information, please email the Special Markets Department at SPsales@harpercollins.com.

FIRST HARPERCOLLINS PAPERBACK PUBLISHED IN 2022

Designed by THE COSMIC LION

Library of Congress Cataloging-in-Publication Data is available upon request.

ISBN 978-0-06-306337-2

22 23 24 25 26 LSC 10 9 8 7 6 5 4 3 2 1

For our parents and friends and people who have helped raise us and who have encouraged and supported our family over the years. We couldn't have done anything without you.

You know what makes me sick to my stomach? When I hear grown people say that kids have changed. Kids haven't changed. Kids don't know anything about anything. We're the ones that have changed.

—**FRANK MARTIN,** *head basketball coach*
at the University of South Carolina

Contents

CONTENTS

10 RULES FOR RESILIENCE

True Resilience

My name is Joe De Sena. I am a father of four and the founder of Spartan, an extreme endurance brand with events in forty-four countries. I like to call us "the Tesla of tough stuff"—innovative, life-changing industry disruptors who put on events that range from obstacle course races to three-mile sprints in elite stadiums to the Spartan Death Race, days and miles of unexpected physical challenges that test participants' character and resilience. Let's be clear: my company is not about building biceps; it's about building better humans. Training, racing, and routine are all a Trojan horse for being *ready for anything*, including life's inevitable challenges.

I am in the business of transformation. My goal is to rip one hundred million people off the couch. I've worked on Wall Street, so trust me when I say there are easier ways to make money. But I discovered through Spartan that I could make an immediate impact on people. I was amazed to see that so many competitors are capable of stepping up and doing the difficult work of preparing mentally and physically for extreme challenges—even those who had seemingly given up on themselves. When given the choice to quit or keep going, many kept going. I was hooked, and Spartan has become a thriving business.

At the start of 2020, the Spartan team and I looked at the year ahead and thought, *This will be the most extraordinary year in the history of the company.* We had just acquired Tough Mudder, a successful obstacle course race company and our competitor for many years. We had booked our Spartan World Championship in Abu Dhabi and had an entire schedule of events slated for every corner of the globe. We had invested in bringing on talented employees in every division of the company. We were primed and ready for a tremendous year of transforming lives and helping our community get stronger, tougher, and more resilient. All the hard work, sacrifices, and time spent away from my family working like an animal were finally paying off.

A kick in the ass wasn't on the agenda. But we most certainly got one. In March 2020, we were forced to cancel every Spartan race planned for that month. *Okay*, I thought, *we'll be back up and running by the summer. We can weather this pandemic storm.* When July rolled around, we canceled the rest of our events for the entire year. This meant not hundreds but thousands of races around the world: thousands of events that Spartan athletes had spent months training for. How could my company—which trains people to *not* social distance or isolate, to come together, get dirty, and get physically and emotionally tough—survive this?

Life doesn't always give you what you want or even what you need. Sometimes it just gives you obstacles to see if you are ready for them. You have two options when you face an unexpected obstacle. You can put your head down and shut out the world, pretend that difficult roadblock isn't there, or you can rise, look up, and take those obstacles head-on.

We did the latter at Spartan, and it has us better positioned and more ready for the future than I could have ever imagined. We made technological innovation changes to our business in only a couple of months in 2020 that I thought would take us years, if they could even happen at all. We held firmly to our mission and sought to reach people with the messages of accountability, change, and discomfort, even if we couldn't bring them together to race. We were forced to simplify, take a long look in the mirror, and do what we do best: persevere. Don't get me wrong. It was hard. We had to rethink how we would do every part of our business in the future, from racing to training to telecommuting.

You might think I hated having all of those hard conversations and facing all of those hard realities as I mapped out an uncertain future for a company I'd given the last two decades of my life to. The truth is, at fifty-two years old, I really enjoy hard stuff. It makes me more resilient, more capable. I know the truth: Everything is hard. Life is hard. Health is hard. Burpees are hard. Eating right is hard. Honesty is hard. Integrity is hard. Changing habits is hard. Parenting is hard.

Because my job puts me in such close contact with people who are desperate to transform their lives, I also have the unique privilege of seeing what else is hard: Obesity is hard. Depression and anxiety are hard. Complacency is hard. Mediocrity is hard.

I tell everyone, *Choose your hard.*

Perhaps the most important lesson that I learned in 2020 is that lessons are everywhere, and if you want to learn, you have to open your eyes and your ears and pay attention.

I believe the reason more people visited the Spartan website in 2020 than ever before—a year when I worried we would go under because no one would seek out the content of a brutal obstacle course company in the middle of a pandemic—is because we teach everyday people how to build a warrior's resilience and to persevere in the face of life's challenges.

But I'll be honest: the word *resilience* has become tough for me. It feels meaningless nowadays because it's been co-opted by every marketing team in every industry to draw customers in. Frankly, so have the words *grit*, *toughness*, and *strength*. Marketing companies would like you to believe that purchasing a T-shirt or product that says RESILIENCE grants you the gift. They want you to think that you can stare at your computer screen, study your way into resilience, and workshop your way into grit. Business blogs want you to think resilience is about "productivity" and "optimization."

No.

I'm here to tell you that resilience is as pure a character trait as they come—you can't buy it, and you don't stumble on it. It takes work. You know it when you've got it. I'm talking about immediately accessible, survival-of-the-fittest, endure-the-pain-and-power-through, adapt-and-respond resilience, the kind you need to protect your health and your family and to stay calm when the world goes to shit. I call it "true resilience."

Resilience is the ability to respond to some kind of adversity as if the adversity didn't happen. It's the ability to press on. Picture an athlete running one hundred miles on dirt trails. At mile 50, the trail is suddenly covered in fresh snow. The resilient runner runs directly into the snowy path and keeps running as if nothing has changed, head down, arms swinging, stride never missing a beat. Despite this new element, this adversity, the runner presses on. What I'm proposing to you in this book is the concept of true resilience, which is the ability to not only walk through adversity but to use it to grow. True resilience looks similar to resilience—our runner is still running directly into the snowy path without missing a beat. But with true resilience, the snow is a welcome sight. The runner sees the snow as an opportunity for growth and uses this new challenge as training for mental toughness and fortitude. The runner stomps through, at full speed, and emerges stronger and tougher than before.

True resilience develops from a body and mind that have been carved out of challenge and failure. True resilience allows you to persevere with confidence and calmness through circumstances most people would consider overwhelming or downright impossible. Yes, you'll use true resilience in the workplace, but also with your family. And it will help you get through health problems, fitness challenges, anxiety, a shifting economy, *everything*. An unexpected terminal illness diagnosis for a loved one or yourself. A job loss. A bad investment of time or money. A breakup or divorce. A partner's irritating habits. An issue with your teenager. A lockdown . . . or, put more plainly, any of the unfortunate, ugly, steep, and daunting mountains of tough stuff that get placed in front of each of us in a lifetime.

The ideas behind true resilience are not new concepts, and they aren't just for adults. Kids embody true resilience better than most adults when given the chance. You can find true resilience baked into the training regimens of Navy SEALs and Olympic athletes and extreme entrepreneurs and even regular people who care about making the most of their one precious life.

True resilience is that special quality you find in the most unbreakable, disciplined people you know—the ones who don't get rattled, who show up early, smile when everyone else starts to stress, and radiate confidence and self-sufficiency. It keeps SEALs from ringing the "I'm out of here" bell during harsh training events meant to break even the hardest body and mind. It gave Spartan warriors the ability to endure strenuous circumstances and painful terrain on the battlefield, which proved essential for victory, even against armies that far exceeded them in number. It allows many of the men and women who run Spartan races to suck it up, get in the mud, crawl under the barbed wire fence, put one foot in front of the other, resist complaining, and even find joy and humor when they are tired, cold, and a little scraped up. True resilience is what propels them to sign up for the next Spartan race, even when they are still sore from the previous one. It is the kind of resilience that embraces—no, *encourages*—adversity. And it is a character trait that I see less and less, even though it is more necessary for navigating the world today than ever before.

A lot of us learn resilience lessons way too late in life. The reason? Humans do not want to feel discomfort. In fact, much of our life is spent seeking comfort. That is our downfall. Our utter devotion to what is safe and comfortable is a crack in our foundation that keeps growing with time, until it is a vast and bottomless abyss—one we can't climb over or out of. The less we allow ourselves to feel discomfort, the less discomfort we can tolerate, until a temperature-controlled bedroom that's one or two degrees off feels unbearable to us, fruits and vegetables don't taste like food because we only eat processed junk, and we can't remember the last time we went for a run (not a jog around the block, a *run*). Resisting discomfort in our own lives is keeping our kids, families, partners, coworkers, parents, friends, and everyone we interact with and influence from knowing the rewards of discomfort, too.

When you snack yourself into a coma, your kids are watching. When you click the television on at 5 p.m. and off at 11 p.m. every night of the week, your kids are watching. When you commit to try something new, like a fitness class or nutrition program, and can't make it through the first week without quitting, you aren't just letting yourself down. When you give up, opt out, or make excuses for why you can't do this or that—even if you don't have kids around to bear witness—what values are you demonstrating for your wife, husband, friends, parents, or roommates? What could you be doing instead of sleeping through your life?

This book was born in 2020, while I watched as families all over the globe faced the discomforts thrust at them and realized how insanely unprepared most people are for difficulty. How we handle challenges defines us and our families. While the entire world was asking, *How do we make things safer for ourselves and our kids?* I was wondering, *How do we make kids more resilient and parents more tough so when this happens again they are ready?* Writing a book about building resilience while so many people in the world are social distancing and wearing masks, guiding their kids through distance learning on laptops and iPads, finding exercise routines that don't require CrossFit gyms and yoga studios, preparing food that doesn't rely on a driver to get it from there to here, and connecting with extended family through glass windowpanes showed me how important it is to practice being uncomfortable even in the best of times. Pandemics don't seem so difficult when you have been embracing discomfort for decades. What's the gift on the other side of discomfort, you ask? True resilience.

To be clear, resilience is not a skill we build to get through a difficult meeting at work or the last five minutes of a workout. That effort is commitment or determination, and, while useful, those are onetime feelings and instincts that allow you to *just keep going.* They have a place in a book about resilience, and you'll see me bring them up throughout these chapters. Most of us can point to a single moment in our life when we persevered. Ask yourself, is that single moment reflective of how I am all the time or how I am *today*? True resilience, as you will come to understand it in these pages, is a skill that serves you in every single challenge (and moment) of your life. True resilience becomes etched in the fabric of your being, a distinct part of your character. It is a gift that keeps giving, as it impacts the way you think about everything, from whether to drive your car (comfortable) or jog (uncomfortable) the three miles to a meeting or appointment, take the kids outside to play even in the rain or in the snow, wake up at 5 a.m. or continue to stay up late watching television and sleep through the alarm, try that hobby or resign to always doing the same old thing.

Stop doing the same old thing. An unbelievable life awaits you and your kids if you give the powerful ideas in this book a chance. If they make you a little uncomfortable, good. They're supposed to. These are the same ideas that have shifted the lives of millions of Spartan athletes and catapulted them to mental fortitude, confidence, and contentment.

I know that I can weather any storm, and I'm confident that my kids can, too. Can you say the same? True resilience is built on a set of rules that I'll outline for you in each chapter of this book. Each of these rules has served me and my family in innumerable ways, and my goal in writing this book is to remind and teach you that it's never too late for you and your family to know true resilience. These are the ten rules for building true resilience:

RULE 1: You Can't, Until You Can

RULE 2: Earned, Not Given

RULE 3: Commit to No Bullshit

RULE 4: Live Your Values

RULE 5: Fail Forward

RULE 6: Dedicate to a Daily Routine

RULE 7: Discipline Breeds Responsibility

RULE 8: Into the Wild

RULE 9: Raw Courage

RULE 10: Ready for Anything

No one can predict when you'll need to access a warrior's resilience, but if 2020 is any indication of the future, resilience will be the single greatest tool available to you and your family as we head into unknown territory. Look around. After resilience, leadership, health, and preparedness are the only survival skills we have. Depression has skyrocketed. Divorce is up. The rate of joblessness is frighteningly high. Ask yourself whether you are ready for what comes next. And if *you* are not, your kids sure as hell are not either.

When I first set out to write *10 Rules for Resilience*, it was out of concern for kids. No one reached out to me more when the pandemic began than parents, concerned that they hadn't prepared their kids for the challenges ahead. As it turns out, they were right. But the kids weren't prepared for the pandemic because their parents weren't prepared.

You will notice as you read this book that I often bring up my own four kids and the kids who have gone through Spartan training camps when I talk about resilience. I bring up family leadership techniques and parenting guidance in almost every conversation I have with adults about resilience. That isn't by accident. Spartans had a belief: train the children to be better than we are. If the next generation isn't stronger than the current generation, then we've failed them and ourselves. Making sure my kids are stronger and more resilient than me has been a mission of mine as a dad from the beginning. That means improving myself as much as I challenge them to improve, and self-correcting when I feel myself sliding into more comfortable patterns. Throughout this book and throughout every chapter, you'll find ways to turn lessons for *you* into lessons for *them*. Every chapter in this book begins with a lesson for you, then shows you how to implement this learning in your family.

Not enough parents even know where to start when it comes to helping their kids build resilience. I won't sugarcoat this for you. The big problem with kids isn't even about the kids—it's about our epic problem as adults. The pendulum has swung so far from authoritative that we don't even act like parents. We kowtow to toddlers: "Oh honey, you don't like spinach lasagna? No problem, let me make you your own meal! And oh, while I'm cooking it, you go ahead and stream your show." We choose what's easy and nonconfrontational, and as I mentioned earlier, we avoid discomfort at all costs—both for ourselves and in the face of our children.

From sugar to sleep, we are wired for indulgence, and we give in to it every time. But temporary feel-good hormones lead to a hard and painful crash when reality finally hits. And how many kids crash when they lose their first job, when a professor doesn't favor them, when they need to work harder to make the team, when they can't see their friends, or when they are forced to keep learning and growing without the pressures of a physical classroom? Unfortunately, kids take after their parents: they avoid discomfort, too. They prefer the couch, they reach for the snack drawer, they report a coach for benching them, they move home, they ask for rent money, they give up.

The headlines about kids struggling with everything from obesity to mental illness to addictions anger me. According to the Centers for Disease Control and Prevention, one in five American kids is obese. Fifteen percent of college students are taking antidepressants. The kids are not alright. But the kids are not the root of the problem; they're the victims of indulgent, spoiled, mindless, soft parenting and a society that would rather spend money selling them vaping tools and video games than making PE a priority in schools. And it's the kids who suffer the consequences. Parents have been complicit with our society's corporatized, commodified laziness (gaming chairs, baby iPad cases . . . it's all BS).

We can—and must—create a tougher generation, starting with our own kids, starting with ourselves. We have to stop discussing issues, writing blogs, and joining more PTA subgroups, and we have to start taking real action. And that action begins with us—the parents.

We can't expect our children to be healthy and resilient humans if we aren't. The incredible, important, and unrelenting job of being a parent isn't best accomplished by following a checklist of how-tos. It's by living and breathing the kind of human that you want your child to be, and then parenting and leading from that same position.

Many of us are exhausted, stressed, and overwhelmed. I get that. But we have to step up. We have to create long-term solutions to seemingly short-term problems. Much of parenting is about the long game. Remember that the children that we are raising today will become the adults that we work with tomorrow. In so many ways, parenting itself is a practice in delayed gratification (an important skill we will talk about later on in the book). Temporary, immediately gratifying solutions may *feel* good now, but are the lessons that your child walks away with the kind that build resilient humans or just more satisfied children?

I have the privilege of interviewing truly amazing people every day. They're unsung heroes, nurses and firemen, as well as billionaires and icons. But what always stands out despite their many differences is that at some crucial point in their lives, they worked extremely hard and overcame obstacles. When I think about what transformed me from a stubborn working-class kid into the founder of a million-dollar company, I go back to the lessons I learned in a rough neighborhood where I failed over and over again, with little help from my tough-as-nails parents.

As a teenager, I started a pool-cleaning service that I eventually sold. For over ten years, as I stood skimming and vacuuming pools for hours on end, I bore witness to the inner workings of about seven hundred homes throughout the five boroughs of New York City. I can tell you, in almost all of the households where the parents indulged their every personal whim, and overprioritized comfort and safety, they suffered personally, and their families suffered in turn. It's not that these adults were negligent. On the contrary, they overprotected, over-supported, and over-helped their kids, and those kids struggled hard. Self-esteem and self-worth were nonexistent. Many got into real trouble, some flunked out of school, and for a few, life took a really bad turn. In contrast, the kids from hardworking families, where the parents clearly valued taking the hard route in their own lives and didn't coddle their young kids, had to get up early, were forced to get an after-school job, and had to take care of younger siblings. These were the kids who tended to excel, grow, and make a good life for themselves. What I saw being a pool cleaner showed me the path to resilience and responsibility, though I might not have realized it at the time: we all need adversity and discipline to meet our best self.

Maybe you had a rough childhood, learned resilience at one point, but lost it when you chose the never-ending comforts of a soft life. So many of us wake up in our thirties or forties realizing we don't recognize ourselves or how we got so sensitive and fragile. We're bored, fatigued, and anxious, but we recognize we have every possible comfort at our fingertips. How is this possible? Whenever I ask someone new to Spartan to tell me the last time they felt alive, they almost always recount an experience when they worked really hard for something. Why, when we reflect on tough experiences, do they seem like the happiest times of our life? Because we were stretching, growing, and feeling all of the pain that comes with discomfort. It's true that challenge is invigorating for humans. Discomfort is like oxygen. True resilience is the reward on the other side that keeps us coming back for more.

This book is 100 percent based on a life lived. It's how I walk through each and every day of my life. I have my flaws and mess up like any other human. I'm not a perfect boss, nor a perfect husband or parent. But my commitment to the rules in these pages is unwavering. Spartan is a community committed to a lifestyle, and in my quest to spark a movement of self-transformation through Spartan and also through writing this book, I've had a lot of collaborators and teachers. One is my coauthor, Dr. Lara Pence, PsyD, the official Spartan Mind Doc. I asked Dr. L to contribute to this project because of her depth of knowledge and authoritative perspective as a longtime psychologist who has helped adults, children, and teens overcome emotional barriers. I never want my advice about helping children to be careless or haphazard. Raising a family has been one of the most resilience-building experiences of my life. However, I also know how utterly wrong our first instincts can be as parents. While I have a lot of stories of transformation and resilience in action, Dr. L has the background and clinical experience to understand and corroborate what is going on beneath the surface. Her influence on keeping these pages grounded in truth has been instrumental.

Agoge (AH-go-GEE) is a word that holds a special place in Spartan history and in my heart. It refers to the ancient Greek rite of passage that transforms a person from a child to a warrior. The word implies leadership, training, and togetherness, and those pillars are the force behind this book you hold in your hands. As we have witnessed through the pandemic, courage and healthy conditioning are about all we can count on. But I promise you, with some hard-won lessons, inviting some healthy failure and turning losses into life lessons, you can prepare yourself and your kids for anything. You can transform yourself from child to warrior, and you can help the people around you do the same. You can start by making your bed and throwing down some burpees. Stop blaming the screens and start showing up and choosing the hard thing. Don't know how? Well, that's the point of this book.

Joe De Sena

A Note from
Dr. Lara Pence

When I first met Joe De Sena, he wasn't wearing shoes. To me, a clinical psychologist who can't help but analyze even the slightest deviation from normal, this seemingly insignificant fact was symbolic. Standing in front of me was a man who turned obstacles into opportunities, removed comfort so others could find courage, and tackled luxury so people could push their limits. Shoes were clearly negotiable.

He stepped into my office to film a piece for a documentary Spartan was making and smoothed his hand across my tufted, blue velvet couch. He warned me with a crooked smile, "You have your work cut out for you, Doc. A lot of people think I'm a maniac." I welcomed the challenge.

I discovered that there is nothing maniacal about Joe at all, although his behaviors are frequently outside the "norm." As his values emerged and his aspirations came to the forefront, it became clear that Joe's mission very much mirrors my own. He wants to change people's lives, and he does so by creating a space where they are challenged to explore and reveal a greater self. Spartan meets therapy. In many ways, a Spartan race is the physical embodiment of what I ask my clients to do daily: tolerate the heavy weight of what's hard, overcome the barriers that stand in their way, and dust off the mud, muck, and grime of life so they can just keep going. Joe and I both work passionately to help people understand that they can do better, and we both agree that if we don't get our act together, our society, and most importantly our kids, will be in deep, deep trouble.

For over fifteen years, I've worked with young children, teenagers, young adults, and their parents in children's hospitals, residential treatment centers, outpatient facilities, and private practice. I've seen how seemingly healthy kids can self-destruct and the toll that it takes on parents. I have counseled mothers and fathers in some of the most dire circumstances: feeding tubes for anorexia, cutting behaviors that led to ICU admissions, violent outbursts that included knives and golf clubs as weapons, hidden bottles of vodka in sock drawers prepuberty, and even completed suicides. But here's the way I see it: The biggest crisis right now is not the rise in mental illness among kids or even childhood obesity rates. It's not the abundance of ADHD in children, the increase in depression among adolescents, or the pervasiveness of panic in young adults. It is the widening circle that pathologizes discomfort, displeasure, and distress as disease. The aforementioned illnesses are indeed trending upward, but we aren't talking about *why*. And the *why* is the problem.

Kids are struggling because parents are struggling. Many are working overtime to make their child's life as easy and comfortable as possible. The relentless pursuit of a happy kid has been joined by the pursuit of ease, thereby stripping children of essential experiences that build patience, tolerance for distress, problem-solving skills, and resilience. While many parents hold the belief that minimizing disappointment, pain, and difficulty makes for a more joyful family, the opposite is proving itself to be true. As more parents pander, they find that their kids are drowning in unpreparedness, mental health issues, obesity, and low self-worth. The trajectory is simple: when you diminish exposure to that which is strenuous, you become incapable of handling that which is tough—otherwise known as life itself. Self-esteem suffers, and resilience reserves become nonexistent. This holds true for both parent and child, which is why building resilient families starts with building resilient parents.

As a mom, I understand the dilemma. We're prewired to protect our young, and discomfort and displeasure can be seen as a threat. When my boys complain or cry, my mom instinct kicks in and I want to scoop them up, hold them tight, and take away whatever is causing distress. Being a psychologist and *knowing* what's better for them doesn't mean that this gets any easier. It's a never-ending exercise in self-evaluation and self-correction, and it's exhausting. And yet it's necessary. My youngest son knows how to make dinner and wash the dishes. He's six. My oldest knows how to do his own laundry and started his own lawn mowing business. He's ten. Both shovel the snow from our sidewalk and the one across the street just for good measure. They're not perfect angels, but they know what hard work means, why commitment is important, and how to adapt when necessary. It hasn't spared them from heartache, tough days, or rough moments, but it has instead given them more tools to get through. But sadly, resilient and self-reliant children like mine are slowly becoming the anomaly.

A few weeks after my first shoeless meeting with Joe, he called me and asked, "Am I crazy?" My response was simple: "Stay the course. Don't do anything different." It was a typical dodge-the-question therapist response, but it was what I wanted him to hear because his work is so vital right now. I've watched Joe with his own kids, and I've watched him with adults. His approach is nearly identical. He challenges his racers to call up resilience, courage, and commitment and to forgo comfort. He encourages his teams at work to face failure and to gain wisdom by learning from past wounds. And he demands that we all get up from the couch and meet our greatest self at the finish line. He asks his kids to do these exact same things every day. His consistency and commitment to these rules of resilience are right at the forefront of who he is as a husband, CEO, and father. His approach might be uncomfortable for some, but that's the point because that's what produces true growth and transformation. As I say to clients all the time, "This is supposed to be uncomfortable. Numbing and the pursuit of comfort got you here. Discomfort will get you out."

Parents often ask me if there is a book I can recommend that will help them become better parents and even better humans. I've longed for something to give them that goes beyond teenage angst, attachment theory, or developmental brain science. Many of these books tell parents what to do, but they miss the key component of whether the parent has the necessary skills in the first place. I've struggled to find a book that reminds parents that their parenting skills will only be as strong as their life skills—one that teaches them how to be better humans first and then how to parent with certain life principles as the guiding light. This is that book, and Joe is the perfect guide. Change starts now, and it starts with you.

You Can't, Until You Can

Build a Better Belief System

> If there is no struggle, there is no progress. . . . This struggle
> may be a moral one; or it may be a physical one; or it may
> be both moral and physical, but it must be a struggle.
>
> —Frederick Douglass

One day a few years ago, I was in New York City preparing for an epic bike trip that I had been planning for months. I was going to ride over three hundred miles on busy streets and back roads from New York City to my farm in Vermont. The route wasn't going to be easy. It was full of steep uphill climbs and a few dangerous curves and downhills, but it would have stunning views all around, and it was the kind of crazy challenge that got me excited. It was going to be a grueling couple of days on the bike, and I was looking forward to the struggle.

The day before I was set to take off, I ran into a friend and his teenage son at a restaurant in NYC. We said our hellos, and I got to talking about my upcoming bike ride. With every tiny description of the hardship ahead, I noticed that the teenager's eyes became wider and wider. They lit up like lightning. His body language shifted from disinterested teenager to curious and energetic young man. He leaned in and made eye contact. There was that undeniable craving in his body for tough stuff—a natural human desire for challenge that I've devoted my life to nurturing within, and sometimes dragging out of, the people I meet. He peppered me with questions: *Where will you sleep?* Wherever seems easiest. *What will you do on roads without bike lanes?* Ride on the edge and hope cars are paying attention. *What will you do if you can't make it up a hill?* Keep going. *What if you blow out a tire? What if your bike breaks down? What if you get hurt? What if you don't have cell phone service? What kind of bike do you have? What are you bringing to eat? Where will you stop for rest?* The questions went on and on.

I was surprised to see this kind of enthusiasm from a kid who not even ten seconds ago barely acknowledged my presence before turning his full attention back to the cell phone in his hand. Even his dad was surprised to see his son's attention redirect. It was as if even the thought of the adventure was breathing life into him.

So I did what I do at Spartan every single day: I leaned in and pushed. "Hey," I said to the kid. "Do you want to come with me? I can get you a bike and gear, no problem."

Silence. A nervous exchange of looks. I stood there, smiling. I watched the familiar dynamic unfold in front of me between parent and child. Hesitation and uncertainty, but, perhaps more important, doubt and fear—all emanating from his dad.

I pushed again. "What do you say? Do you want to bike three hundred miles with me? It's gonna be really fun."

Suddenly my friend jumped in: "Oh, I don't think so, Joe. He's never done anything like this before. It's way too long of a ride for him. I don't know about him sleeping somewhere in the middle of nowhere at night, and we have plans tonight and tomorrow. Besides, I can't even remember the last time he rode a bike. He would slow you down. Maybe next time."

Why kick off the first chapter of a book on resilience with this story? If you want to be resilient and if you want to build resilience in your family or any of the people around you, which you must because you picked up a book called *10 Rules for Resilience*, you have to start *noticing*. I don't mean passive noticing. I mean intense awareness of the thoughts running through your brain, your patterns of thought, and how those thoughts eventually come out of your mouth and convert into action. *You are your thoughts.* Every great athlete, entrepreneur, leader, or parent that I've ever encountered begins by looking at how they think and at the limitations those thoughts are placing on themselves and others. Thoughts are your first obstacle.

You know that feeling you get before you head into a big meeting or presentation? The minutes leading up to the meeting, which were barely noticeable to you an hour ago, now feel electric—two minutes until go time, one minute until go time, a few seconds, okay, ready, aim, *fire.* You are suddenly aware of every ping-ponging thought because suddenly every one of them matters. That's how aware you need to be as you begin to train yourself for resilience. Notice the thoughts running through your head, the words coming out of your mouth, the work you're putting in, and where you are on the road to where you want to be. Is the narrative in your head one of constant fear? Are you entering every room and every conversation thinking you're an impostor? Are you defensive, jumpy, and unreliable? Do you think more about what you're doing wrong instead of what you're doing right? What are you thinking *right now*?

Be aware that your thoughts affect your family. Notice the limitations you place on yourself, because what you tell yourself is what your family, kids, and spouse will start to tell themselves, too. *I'm not strong enough. I don't have enough money. I'm unprepared. I can't.*

Do you want your family to have the same thoughts running through their heads that you do? If not, it's time to change. Now that you're noticing what's happening in your mind, it's time to put that unhelpful voice on mute.

Difficult Versus Desperate

One of the fundamental obstacles to resilience is mistaking what is difficult for what is desperate. A difficult situation is a growth opportunity. If you want true resilience, you need to put yourself in difficult situations every single day. That means striving for more items off that to-do list at work, more burpees today than you did yesterday, more presence in the here and now by dedicating to longer meditations or committing to whatever that thing is that you want to do better.

A desperate situation is different. It's a survival situation, a life-or-death situation.

I see the push and pull between difficult and desperate in action at Spartan when new racers, both adults and kids, come to the farm to train for the first time. Most of these new athletes genuinely have no idea what they are capable of, so at some point in the middle of a training session, their brain starts telling them things that aren't true. They give up at the point of "difficult"—way, way, way before they get to the point of "desperate." I have no doubt that they *think* their situation is desperate. Their brains are saying, *It's impossible. I can't do this*. But the truth is, it's only difficult.

How can you tell the difference?

When that struggle begins between brain and body, the newbie I'm working with tends to walk sort of timidly over to me. I've seen it a hundred times, and I know exactly how this conversation is going to go. They will say, "I quit. I can't. I'm done."

I'll say, "Okay, you can go. But try this first. Turn off that voice in your brain and for the next five minutes just put your head down and put one foot in front of the other. Do that, and if you want to quit afterward, fine."

It sounds simple, and we've all heard it a thousand times. But many miss the key takeaway: separating what's difficult from what's desperate—telling yourself, *This isn't desperate. I'm not dying. I'm just doing something difficult with my body.* That's how you start to determine the difference—if you can put one foot in front of the other and maintain that separation, then believe me, you can keep going.

So what is going on in our brains? What the heck is the matter with them if they tell us to stop before we even get started? That is a topic that we'll revisit in future chapters. My experience is that whenever we do something we've never done before, when we cross a threshold into unknown territory, our brains jump in with well-intentioned concern. Many Spartans who run our races are climbing a rope for the first time or running their fourth mile when they've never run more than three. So the brain is telling the body, *Wait, wait, wait! I don't like this. I don't know what's going to happen if I keep going. This feels like a threat.* And when our brain interprets something as threatening, it sends signals for us to stop. It's then that the task at hand starts to look humungous because as the difficulty of the next step intensifies, the difficulty of step 10 or 20 feels impossible. So it's important to remember that big tasks are accomplished with small movements. This reminds me of a piece of wisdom I like to tell others when they are starting something new and challenging:

How do you eat an elephant?

One bite at a time.

The most pernicious thoughts that we can have are the ones that limit us because when thoughts limit what we think we can do, then they have greater power over limiting what we actually do. And it gets worse: they can also limit what we think others can do. There are two important takeaways from the bike story I shared earlier. First, stop putting limitations on yourself. Second, stop putting limitations on your kids.

My friend rightfully didn't want to put his son in a desperate position where his life would be threatened. (Unfortunately, I know first-hand that desperate feeling from a time I was trapped on the side of a mountain in a blizzard.) So my friend's paternal instincts kicked in — this bike ride could be a threat to his son's very life, and that is unacceptable. But a long, difficult bike ride with an experienced rider and adult is not the same as an approaching lion or a semitrailer swerving into your lane or being stuck on the side of a mountain in a blizzard without food or water. It is a challenge, simple as that, and we need to struggle through challenges in order to grow.

How do we learn to stop putting limitations on our kids? It all comes down to fear. When you understand why fear is there in the first place (to protect against threats) and you recognize that the threat isn't real, then you can notice — truly notice — whether you are limiting the people around you instead of allowing them to grow. I like to think of it in terms of the opposite of limiting: encouraging. My strategy is that I know I'm never limiting my family if I'm always encouraging them to do difficult things. If, when challenging opportunities arise for the people in my life, I'm doing my best to encourage them toward those challenges (as uncomfortable as this sometimes can be), I can rest assured I'm not doing the opposite: imposing limitations.

Perhaps most importantly, never put limitations on yourself. Honor your own personal desire for challenges. With comforts of every kind at our fingertips, we have fewer and fewer reasons to challenge ourselves in life. Most of us will take obvious paths to career, health, and family. We go to college, major in something normal, get an entry-level job, and keep going until we have a mortgage and a family and a 401(k). We exercise a little bit and maybe aspire to retire early or own a vacation home. Sure, there are some typical challenges on this path, but rarely do we feel that zest for a grand, extraordinary challenge, to do something extremely uncomfortable and difficult.

My advice is simple: when you feel it, *go for it*. If you feel that urge to train for a marathon, don't think about it—just sign up. If you're looking longingly at that route at the climbing gym that always seemed way beyond your skill set, hop on. If an assignment at work sounds stimulating, volunteer for it, even if it is above your pay grade. Hell, quit your job and start that company you're dreaming about. If you want to bike three hundred miles on a single day's notice, even though you are a teenager and you don't know anything about long-distance biking, don't let anything stop you, not even your dad. Other people's doubts say nothing about your abilities. Their limitations are not your limitations.

Your own doubts and fear can become the biggest obstacle you will ever encounter, which is why I put this chapter first. You can't, until you can. So much of this is about the stories you tell yourself and the words you speak in your head. The mind is a powerful thing. Limitations come from simple phrases like "I can't" or "I'm not ready." The more you tell yourself these things, the more you will believe them. Don't let your own insecurities be the road map for how you live your life. Negative thinking patterns and self-limiting beliefs exist in all of us, but you choose what you want to pay attention to. Which will you choose? The voice that tells you, *Don't do it. You probably can't*, or the one that says, *You've got this. Why the fuck not?* I know which one I listen to, and it's served me pretty well in life. It's not always easy, but easy doesn't reveal greatness.

As you'll learn in this book, the keys to true resilience are hard work, failure, and action. Therefore, the opposite of true resilience is doing nothing at all, being successful in opting out and achieving the least. Trust me, this is never the path to a great life. And I mean *never*. When you act, you have data. You can learn, change, and grow. The son's acceptance to do nothing, to let his dad speak for him, won't work for him if he wants to weather storms in his future. He'll need proof of experience—resilience data points, or RDPs, as Dr. L calls them—showing that he can accomplish tough stuff and work through difficult, strenuous situations. He'll need to be aware of his weaknesses—body and mind—so he can strengthen them. Without action, he knows as much about himself today as he did yesterday. If this path continues long into the future, as it does for many adults, he could wake up a decade later with no true sense of himself and be unprepared for even the lightest storm life throws his way. This is why we have to pay attention to what's circulating in our brains and tackle it head-on.

The happy ending to this story? I kept pushing and pushing, and father and son rose to the occasion. The father gave his blessing, and the son stepped up and met the challenge.

That's right, the teenage son biked over three hundred miles with me without a single day of training under his belt. He even did it on a borrowed bike! Yes, it was difficult. Yes, it was even painful at times. Yes, he felt more alive than he'd ever felt before.

And yes, it was fun.

The Parable of the Elephant

For hundreds of years, elephant trainers have used a technique to control their elephants. They'll take a baby elephant and tie one of its legs to a post with a rope. The young elephant will struggle for days to escape, violently thrashing and pulling on the rope. Eventually, it will realize that the rope is too great an opponent and will simply stop trying. It has learned that the length of this rope is the full extent of its range of motion and freedom.

Later, when that elephant has grown to full size and could easily break through the rope with one swing of its leg, it won't even try to escape. There's a well-known term in psychology for this phenomenon: it's called "learned helplessness." The elephant has learned that struggle against the rope is useless, and it will move no farther than the length of that rope, convinced that the same opponent that defeated it years ago can defeat it today.

We often think incorrectly that resilience is something we build as we grow up and age. The truth is that true resilience is within us from birth, but we cultivate it through life experience and bring it to the forefront with challenge and circumstance. Sadly, resilience is something we *unlearn* in our modern world—and then must learn again when we dedicate ourselves to building it, like you're doing with this book. Human infants, for example, are helpless in innumerable ways. But if you've ever been around infants as they grow into toddlers, you'll see that testing limits (like learning to walk) and fearless exploration (like picking up new toys) are something babies move toward, not away from. It isn't until Mom or Dad step in, swooping the child up with "No, no, not yet," that these traits begin to go underground. It is helplessness that we learn, like the baby elephant. And we learn it by overprotecting ourselves and overprotecting others, especially children.

Ask yourself, *Am I living my life like the baby elephant?* Consider whether there are ropes that you could easily break through but have learned to tolerate as shackles to your current circumstance.

Furthermore, are you teaching your kids learned helplessness with an invisible rope, tethering them to a life that is less than what it should be? This is an important question to explore because scientists have found a clear correlation between learned helplessness and low self-esteem—in adults and children. When you impose limitations on the people around you, you're indirectly telling them that they are incapable of handling hardship on their own.

Resilience and Limitations

The strength of your personal resilience and the strength of your self-imposed limitations are directly proportional. You can measure resilience by measuring limitations. Let's take a triathlete, for example. Suppose this athlete practices swimming only in a temperature-controlled pool in a gym.

The race arrives and the requirement is miles of swimming in open water in a lake or a bay. The water is dark and murky. There is a psychological element to swimming with a vast and deep stretch of natural water below. The water is freezing and constricts the athlete's muscles. And then there are other elements, like smell, wind, waves, and weather. The limitations of a perfectly constructed, crystal-clear swimming pool impact the athlete's mental and physical toughness in the open water.

I still commend this athlete for endurance training in a swimming pool, don't get me wrong. But if you want true resilience, the ability to survive whatever life throws at you, you have to get uncomfortable eventually. You have to trust that you can get out of the swimming pool and into the lake. Then you have to get out of the lake and jump into the ocean. Raising the bar for yourself is where you get the best return on investment. By giving yourself an opportunity to meet challenges head-on, you allow yourself to demonstrate your greatness. The fewer the limitations that you put on yourself, the greater the opportunities you'll have to cultivate that true resilience.

You Can't, Until You Can

We've focused a lot in this chapter on limitations. Now, how can you get rid of them? You can't. Not completely. It's not about eliminating all limitations from your life; it's about having them but finding a way through by opting in to a challenge rather than opting out.

I hate to sound like a cliché, but here goes: you can do anything. I really mean that.

How do I know? Because I see it every year when hundreds of thousands of people who think to themselves, *There's no way I can do a Spartan race*, show up on the starting line and cross the finish line. And because I've done it myself.

I first learned about physical fitness, Ironman triathlons, and ultramarathon races during my time working in finance on Wall Street. I was sedentary all day long for the first time in my life, working eighty-hour weeks and stressed beyond belief.

I've documented this story a few times, so I won't bore you with the details, but in short, I met a man in the stairwell of my apartment building, and he was running the stairs. Eventually I joined him, and the rest is history.

Soon I was competing at the highest level in extreme endurance races. But the time between is important. It started by challenging myself to do something for three minutes. Then, pretty soon, I was challenging myself to thirty minutes. Now what about thirty days?

It seems like a stretch, but this is how every goal I've ever achieved came to be, abandoning the idea of limiting myself in favor of challenging myself. If you say yes to challenges everywhere you see them, you'll achieve beyond your wildest dreams.

You Can't, Until You Can: For the Family

ENCOURAGE YOUR FAMILY TO ACCOMPLISH HARD SHIT

COVID-19 has reminded us that adversity is part of being human. We can't control the challenges that life will set before us, and you don't have to manufacture adversity for it to land in your lap. We can, however, prepare ourselves to adapt to the toughest times—and even to lead others through them. Maybe that's why, driving home from Spartan's first post-lockdown event last spring, the idea of adding a Death Race for kids hit me like a lightning bolt. Many of our children are too unprepared for tough times, and I wanted to give my children and others a reference point so they could understand their own strength in the face of difficulty. Kids, like adults, need to practice pushing their own limits. So I began calling friends and family with an offer for their kids to attend a fourteen-day summer camp with my kids at our farm in Pittsfield, Vermont.

The twenty-two kids, ages eight to eighteen, who showed up on my doorstep expected a two-week summer farm camp, lifting bales of hay and hiking trails, but they got something akin to fourteen days of Delta Force instead. My team included ethnobotanist Sefra Alexandra, Olympic wrestler Andy Hrovat, and mountain warfare veteran Eric Ashley. The participants woke up with the rooster at 6 a.m. the first day, getting up earlier and earlier each day that followed until they were up at 4:45 a.m. We made them hike up mountains carrying heavier and heavier rocks, in the heat, over and over, each day. We challenged them to plunge into and under the icy White River. We taught them that *on time is late* and that *details matter*. We removed processed crap from their diets. We required them to memorize and recite Theodore Roosevelt's "Man in the Arena." (Here's my favorite line: "Credit belongs to the man who is actually in the arena, whose face is marred by dust and sweat and blood; who strives valiantly; who errs, who comes short again and again, because there is no effort without error.")

Every kid cried, fell down, hit the ground, and said, "I can't." My reply was, "You can't *yet*." We took their phones away during the day, but some of the texts they sent their parents at night were telling and hilarious, along the lines of:

> *Get me out of here.*
> *This guy is a crazy person.*
> *They make us cry in the cold river.*
> *SOS. Help!*
> *You have sent your son to Hell.*

My wife, Courtney, and I got phone calls from concerned and sometimes enraged parents. I told them they'd be doing their children a disservice if they didn't let them finish the hard shit they had started. The kids were a little cold, a little hungry at times, but fed, safe, and sleeping in nice indoor spaces.

There was a girl named Emma McLaughlin whom I pushed extra hard. She's a brilliant kid, a straight-A student. However, her dad, a friend of mine, had started to worry as Emma got older. She'd never done a push-up or a sit-up, let alone a burpee. The more comfortable she got resisting physical challenges, the less she could endure. That's a pattern that repeats itself over and over for all of us at every stage of life. At thirteen, she started to lack confidence, which her dad, Brian, noticed in her posture, voice, and "shrugging shoulders."

For the first three days of the camp, Emma cried pretty much nonstop. "Please, I'll do anything to get home," she texted her parents. "I can't do this. There's no point to this." Her parents say it was tough to ignore her pleas, but they didn't respond. Every day, as she chopped wood, climbed under barbed wire, foraged, and carted sandbags, she, along with her teammates, got a little stronger, a little tougher. There was a moment on day 4 when she was carrying a younger child on her back down the mountain. She kept yelling out that she didn't think she would make it, but she did, and something changed in her. The crying stopped.

By the end of the second week, all the campers stayed in the cold river longer than they had during week 1, of their own volition. Emma's transformation, however, was the most phenomenal. As she discovered her own strength, her own self-imposed limitations began to fade, and she felt more empowered. She proved to herself that she could do a hell of a lot more than push-ups. I watched her become a true athlete and leader. She smiled through the pain. She motivated the other kids through the Death Race, the grueling, eighteen-hour finale of the camp, even as I dared her to quit. She stared back at me with pure grit in her eyes. Yeah, I'm a hard-ass, but watching this girl's transformation moved me and reminded me why I started Spartan in the first place:

physical accomplishments, like finishing a Spartan race, translate into confidence in every aspect of your life. You'd think after the hell I put these kids through that none of them would want to do it again, but most of them thanked me at the end and asked to come back. It turns out that bragging rights are a great motivator. More important, conquering the Death Race is a story these kids get to incorporate into their ideas about themselves.

Like the teenager who biked three hundred miles with me from New York City to Vermont, some of the kids who attended our camp had been shielded from challenge for their entire lives. That's no exaggeration. I meet kids at my summer camp whose parents have limited and limited and limited them, until, like Emma, they stare at a river they should be pumped to jump into to get covered in mud and feel free, but they don't think they can do it. They have been protected and helped instead of being challenged to step outside of what is comfortable or safe. They'd never been allowed to push their own limits and fall down. Some had developed the idea that they couldn't do the hard thing, until an opportunity showed them that they could. They can. They will.

WHAT EXACTLY IS OVERPARENTING?

I realize my mental toughness training for my kids is an outlier in the world of helicopter parenting, snowplow parenting, bubble-wrap parenting, and rampant perfectionism, but the pendulum needs to shift because too many American kids are suffering from this epidemic of overparenting.

Overparenting develops from a misguided belief that kids are fragile—like little china teacups—and that the world outside the front door is a dangerous and deadly environment from which we must protect them. Overparenting overlaps a lot with overprotecting. Over time, overparenting results in human beings who are ill-prepared to deal with, adapt to, and overcome the trials and tribulations of living.

Once when my family was in Montauk, I was coaching five-year-old Charlie through a mile swim across a lake. I was swimming beside Charlie, who was wearing a life vest, struggling a bit, and only a quarter mile from greatness. A woman on a dock started screaming for me to pull him out of the water, and eventually she rowed her kayak out to confront me. I told her my kid was fine (and a few other things). And you know what? He was. Charlie finished the swim, because in our family, we finish what we start. That victory belonged to Charlie. If I had assumed he couldn't make it, carried him in, and wrapped him in a towel, how would that have impacted his self-image? Coddling him because what he was doing was hard and stressful would have set him back.

In their book, *The Coddling of the American Mind*, authors Greg Lukianoff and Jonathan Haidt argue that our modern obsession with protecting children from feeling unsafe can be linked to a steep rise in depression, anxiety, and suicide rates among teens. "When we overprotect children, we harm them," they write. "We make it far more likely that those children will be unable to cope with such events when they leave our protective umbrella." Kids raised this way grow to be emotionally and physically unprepared for life. We've got to reframe our thinking if we want our kids to have a fighting chance at a fulfilling existence.

Scrapes, scabs, and bloody knees; stress; discomfort; feelings of anxiety, rejection, and disappointment; stepping out of the safety zone—all of these need to be reframed from the negative to the positive. From limitation to critical life lesson. Think about this: When you stress a muscle with resistance exercise, the tiny fibers of that muscle tear and break down. Then they grow bigger and stronger as those fibers repair themselves. When you run, the pounding of every foot strike makes your bones denser and stronger. The skeletal system becomes less fragile, not more. When your child's immune system is exposed to a germ, it learns how to fight it off faster the next time and becomes stronger. Experience makes the mind stronger. By not overprotecting your kids, by doing less for them, you will make your children more resilient in response to the unpredictable world.

Take it from Rocky Balboa: "The world ain't all sunshine and rainbows. It's a very mean and nasty place." Rocky may be a fictional character, but the truth hurts. If we want to prepare our kids for this world, we need to be tough enough to exert *less* control over their lives. How do you know if you are overparenting and/or limiting your kids' life experiences? Consider your relationship to risk.

RISK-TAKING

We all know that feeling of watching our children take their first step. We've released our hand from their tiny fingers, watched them wobble, and then witnessed their first demonstration of true independence. Small step for baby, giant leap for parenting, right? Right.

Yet so often I see parents restrain their children from possible risk. They say no to letting the child climb the tall ladder at the playground and instead offer the smaller structure as an alternative. They discourage a new sport in favor of a safer activity. They stop their kids from applying to a "reach" college and recommend a more "attainable" school. And yes, they respond with "Maybe next year" when their kid asks to run a Spartan race. What's at play here? Why do parents do that?

Two primary reasons: First, we are wired to see risk as a threat. Our brain steps in and says, *No, no, no. Let's not do that.* But bubble-wrapping doesn't serve anyone, least of all your kids. Second, risk is uncertain. And not knowing the outcome can be enough for parents to discourage kids. Neither of these reasons, however, are *good* reasons . . . they're just reasons. Avoidance of threats and fear of the unknown are part of being human, but we don't have to go along with them just because our old wiring says we should.

As parents, we need to make risk less taboo. We have to let our children take risks. When we discourage risk and prohibit our kids from stretching themselves, not only do we take away an opportunity for them to build self-esteem but we inadvertently send them the message that we don't think they can do it. And believe me, they pick up on that message. Dr. L has sat with many kids who have been limited and discouraged from doing one thing or another, and what they often tell her is that they feel sad that no one believes in them, has faith in them, trusts that they can do it. Who is "no one"? Their parents. Even if the message that is being received is unintentional, it is still being received, and it etches its way into a child's self-esteem.

And what if these kids really *can't* do it, what if they're encouraged and they fail anyway? Isn't there tremendous benefit in allowing them to try? I think so. Doing so gives them an opportunity to pick themselves up and try again. I call it "failing forward," and we'll talk about it later in the book. Remember your children's first step forward? They fell at some point, right? And what happened next? They tried to stand up once more. They failed forward. Letting your children take risks gives them an opportunity to rise when they fall. And there is tremendous wisdom to be gained from any failure, no matter how big or small.

Here are two exercises to try with kids that will help both you and them begin to challenge those limits.

Push Them out of Their Comfort Zones

Struggle reveals character and builds confidence. You know this, but your kids don't. So sometimes—for their own good—you need to push them when they won't budge. "We know that being able to tolerate discomfort is a wonderful life trait, and in addition to that, it makes them grittier and more resilient," says child and adolescent psychiatrist Harold S. Koplewicz, MD, the founding president of the Child Mind Institute. A child really feels a sense of accomplishment and pride when he or she gets through something tough. As a parent, you want your kids to experience that feeling.

How hard should you push? Only you know your kids and how hard you can nudge them forward. That being said, remember your own limiting beliefs or fears. You may *feel* that they can only be pushed slightly, but ask yourself, *Am I afraid of pushing because I'm afraid they may fail or experience distress?* One way to move forward slowly if you have a more hesitant child is by using a technique called "scaffolding," where you ease your child into it by gradually dispelling his or her fears. Let's say your daughter is anxious about going out for the soccer team and is dead set against attending that first practice. You might go walk the practice field with her a few days before the start. Meet with the coach. Arrange for your kid to talk with someone who played on the team last season. Read a book or watch a video about soccer. Pushing her to take these tiny steps out of her comfort zone will show her that she can get through it even if she experiences butterflies before that first practice.

Be Firm About Commitment

One of the mistakes many parents make that reinforce self-limitations and fear avoidance is allowing their kids to quit when the going gets tough. If you give them a way out, they'll never learn how to persevere to beat fear. While helping your children by pushing them out of their comfort zone, you also want to teach them that if they make a commitment, they have to stick to it. Getting scolded by the piano teacher for not practicing scales is not an acceptable reason to bail. Being moved from first-string tailback to second-string does not give your child a pass to quit the team. Feeling nervous about the upcoming school play is not an excuse to miss theater practice. You may have to get tough if you want your kids to cultivate courage, so stand firm. Teach them the value of fulfilling their commitments even when things don't go their way. If you let them bail because they are in distress, you reinforce the feedback loop that the best way to feel better is to remove discomfort and engage in self-limiting behaviors. If this becomes the lens through which they begin to see the world, then they will avoid anything difficult because they will know that this is an effective strategy to avoid uncomfortable feelings. Remember, the goal is building resilience, not making your kid smile at every turn.

Finish What You Start
Carola Jain

Carola Jain, former chief marketing officer of Spartan, has been sending her three children to Spartan camps for years, but in 2020 when she sent her eldest, Timin, age twelve, to the Agoge Camp that culminated in a Death Race, the experience challenged her resolve and forced her to make hard choices.

My son Timin had been going to Vermont for his annual summer camp with the De Sena kids for years, so we decided I'd go up to the farm and drop Timin there for an impromptu kids camp that Joe had set up last minute. We drove up early Monday morning, and the first thing I saw were all the campers in the river. While it was warm outside, the river was ice-cold, and the kids were told to keep their heads under water for a long period. Timin goes surfing in Long Island often and isn't one to complain about the cold. He was really shivering, and the counselors were calling for him to go back under. I told myself, *You have to go; you can't see this.* So I caught up with Timin later in the wrestling room to say goodbye, and I could see that he was leery of the week ahead. He didn't ask to leave, but he said, "Mom, why don't you stay here in Joe and Courtney's house, and I'll stay with you?"

It was difficult to leave him at that moment, but I knew it would be good for him to get out of his comfort zone, so I gave him a hug, told him we would see him that coming weekend, and left.

On Wednesday night, Timin somehow borrowed another kid's phone and called me: "Mom, please come and get me by Friday. I don't see the point of doing the twenty-four-hour event on Friday. Every day, we're dragging rocks up the mountain, earlier and earlier. Today we got up at 4 a.m. I'm happy to stay until Friday, but I really don't want to do this Death Race."

I spoke with my husband. We told Timin, "You made a commitment of five nights, and you should stick it out." However, I did put in a call to Joe to tell him that Timin had seemed distressed and maybe he should check in and see how he was doing.

The result of this call, and the other parents' calls, was that Joe decided to take all the kids' phones away. He sent a message to the parents, saying, "Parents, *you* are the problem."

This was painful. I didn't want my child to feel that we were not responding to his request for help. Joe told me, "You have a really strong kid, but he arrived with an extra layer of bubble wrap." This struck a chord with me. You see, Timin is very strong willed, and we are a very cuddly family. My husband and I decided Timin would tough it out. Joe has known Timin for years, and I knew that he would be very hard on him, yet with his best interest in mind.

Because that is what Joe does: he makes it his

challenge to help people discover their own best by having them meet themselves in adversity. I wanted my son to meet himself during his stay up there this summer.

The Death Race started at 4 a.m. on Friday morning. I got a call from Joe, who told me Timin tapped out at 1 a.m., *twenty-one hours* after he began. There had been only one climb left. Timin went up the mountain three or four times. The kids had been blindfolded, they were barefoot, and they followed a small path that they had laid the day before in preparation for the race. Timin had simply refused to do the final climb up the mountain. He had stretched out, wet and exhausted, on the floor of Joe's barn and had gone to sleep. He wasn't the only kid who had quit. There were several before him and some after him.

When Joe called me in the morning, he told me he didn't want Timin to finish the race that way. He knew he had more inside of him. In the morning, Joe wanted to give all of the kids who had quit one more opportunity to do the final hike and finish the race that way. Timin flatly refused. He said he just wanted to go home. He got on the phone with me and told me there was no point.

Our family is close to the De Senas, so the plan all along was for Joe to drive Timin home to our house in Long Island. Joe worked on Timin that entire ride from Vermont to Long Island. He told him he could finish the race by walking for hours on the beach from Montauk to Southampton. At first, Timin refused. Joe said to him, "My job is for you to finish. I am not giving up on you." Just before they reached Long Island, they came up with another idea of how he would finish the race.

They decided that they would extend the camp another day and get up early on Sunday morning and walk three miles back and forth on the beach in Southampton, carrying a heavy, forty-pound chain. Joe's sons agreed to join Timin in his last step to "graduate" from the Death Race.

When Timin got home, he told me that the Death Race was the worst thing that ever happened to him and that he didn't want to have anything to do with Joe De Sena ever again. He ate a chocolate croissant, and he said that was the best thing he had ever tasted.

The next morning, all of us—Joe, my husband, Timin, and Joe's boys—went to the beach at 5:30 a.m. so Timin could finish his race. He carried forty-pound chains with his siblings and friends back and forth on the beach until he finished. We walked beside him. When we made it back, about four hours later, Joe was satisfied and said Timin had graduated from the Death Race.

Although on Saturday Timin had let me know he never wanted to do a Death Race again, when we sat down for lunch on Sunday (only three hours after Joe had left), he said, "By the way, I hear they are doing another Death Race with parents in a month. Can we go? Can I bring my friends?"

I was shocked. I said, "I thought you said you'd never do that again."

Timin shrugged and said, "It wasn't that bad. And by the way, I don't think you or dad could ever do it."

I saw the psychology in action. My son went from hating the experience to being proud of himself. He realized he's more capable than he thinks.

We have all learned this: you can't be defined by the time you fell; you have to be defined by the time you got up and finished.

In Conclusion

So I ask you, are you living your life staring at the murky lake, afraid to jump in? Are you an adult elephant being held back by a meaningless rope? Have your own perceived limitations filtered down to your kids? Are you teaching them learned helplessness? You can't train your kids away from this mentality if you succumb to it time and time again.

This chapter is all about limitations: the ones you put on yourself and the ones you put on your kids. Why start with limitations when coaching you on building resilience in yourself and in your family? Because, unfortunately, we are going to have to knock some shit down in that brain of yours and clear away a foundation before we can start building.

For most people, there is a poorly built structure on the surface of your mind—it was built by instinct throughout your life as you learned the wrong way to handle situations, then enforced those patterns of thought and behavior. You've likely been using that failing structure to guide your choices no matter what state of disrepair it is in. Perhaps you thought you could build resilience by simply fortifying the current structure you have, adding some planks of wood here and there. The truth is, you can't. You're going to have to knock that house down and rebuild one brick at a time. When my wife, Courtney, and I bought a farm in Vermont, I wanted to create a whole new foundation for the barn that we were renovating. Contractors and concrete suppliers told me that I didn't need as strong and stable a structure as I was asking for. "It's like you're building a Walmart or something that will be here forever." That's exactly what I wanted, though: a strong foundation on which we could build our new life together. You've got to want the same for yourself as you learn more about true resilience. We've got to get the foundation right before we can build upward.

Small wins grow into big gains for both you and your kids. The "You Can't, Until You Can" attitude isn't all about grand, sweeping, life-altering changes. Sometimes it's just about doing the smaller hard stuff, too. Getting up on a gloomy, rainy, stay-inside-and-watch-TV kind of day and heading out for a walk. Or telling the kids to fold the laundry for the first time. The point is, you must become more aware of what state your mind is in and then change the way you think, behave, and act in accordance with where you want to be, not where you are today. This is not going to be easy, but you can do it. True resilience arrives as you do regular maintenance on that new structure, continuing to test it for cracks and weak spots.

Earned, Not Given

The Power of Hard Work
and Delayed Gratification

> While all excesses are hurtful, the most dangerous is un-
> limited good fortune. It excites the brain, it evokes fancies
> in the mind and clouds in deep fog the boundary between
> falsehood and truth.
>
> —Seneca (5 BC–AD 56), *De Providentia*

When I was living in Ithaca, New York, and was about to graduate from high school, I wasn't sure I wanted to go to college. I was already running a pool-cleaning business that was doing great, and I didn't really see the point of four more years of school. However, my buddy was applying to Cornell and told me he was sure we could get in "no problem" because his dad was a professor. He encouraged me to apply as well, and so without giving it much thought, I filled out an application and went through the interview process. Coming from a Queens neighborhood filled with Mafia,

I thought this "I got a guy" mentality made sense, though it was far from how the real world worked, as I would find out.

Of course, we both got rejected. My grades sucked, so I didn't deserve to get in. But then, after being rejected, college became . . . enticing. That failure ignited something in me. If this college admissions thing couldn't be hacked and I had to actually qualify for it, I wanted to know that I had it in me to get in, whatever it took. All of a sudden, I wanted to go to Cornell.

This is true for me (and I've discovered it is true for the majority of people who work with me at Spartan): if you tell me I can't, I'll show you I will. Failure is where true resilience begins, and we've dedicated an entire chapter to it later in this book.

At the time I was applying to Cornell, even if you weren't accepted to a college, you could enroll as a nonmatriculated student and start taking classes. Those classes would count as credits if you eventually got in or if you were accepted to another school. I only had eyes for Cornell, and I knew I would have to convince them to let me in based on my hard work and success as a nonmatriculated student. I spent my summer enrolled in three classes, learning how to study while running my pool-cleaning business. My buddy went to Vegas and partied; I buckled down. I ended up performing really well in these classes, and I actually got good grades. Confident that I had figured it out, I applied again. I remember the feeling I had after that first semester when I saw that I had straight As. I felt like a shoo-in! I felt as if I deserved to be enrolled as a Cornell student. Look at all the work I'd done! Look at all of my growth!

Here's the thing. How I feel about what I deserve has absolutely nothing to do with what it takes to truly earn something. For example, consider March 2020. As mentioned, at Spartan we had prepared ourselves to have an amazing year of races. We had made big investments, which at the time looked impressive, lucrative, and smart. We put thousands of hours into those decisions and plans. I felt as if we *deserved* success, as if we deserved the rewards from our labor. Well, the year 2020 didn't give a shit about what I felt my company deserved. The rules changed, success had a new set of criteria, and if I wanted success in 2020, I was going to have to earn it.

This is especially true for athletes. In 2018, Michele Graglia finished the Badwater 135, a grueling 135-mile course that begins in the Badwater Basin of California's Death Valley, in 24 hours and 51 minutes, taking the first-place trophy. Naturally, every athlete training to compete the next year assumed Michele's time was the one to beat if they wanted first place. Well, they were wrong. In 2019, Yoshihiko Ishikawa completed and won the Badwater 135 in just 21 hours and 33 minutes. While the second-place time of 24 hours and 13 minutes did indeed beat Graglia's time from 2018, it only merited second place in 2019. The bar became higher, and the expectations moved. Athletic competition, winning, and trophies don't give a shit about your feelings. They are pure in that sense. It doesn't matter what you think you *deserve*; it matters what you *earn*.

As you've probably guessed by now, I got rejected from Cornell the second time I applied. Each year the admissions process grew more rigorous, the competition fiercer. I was going to have to treat this like a test of endurance and mental fortitude, not a sprint. I worked my ass off juggling my company and classes for another semester. I applied, and again I got rejected. I did it again, until finally, I got into Cornell on my fourth try. When I accomplished this, I felt like pounding my chest. Thank God I had to work for it. When I got into college, the accomplishment was mine, and it meant something.

I tell this story in almost every interview I do because this experience was a huge learning moment in my life, and it set me on a course to mental toughness and true resilience. It also showed me that not everyone has what it takes to win, and sometimes that person is looking me in the mirror. My friend who partied in Vegas while I was working full days and studying at night never got into Cornell. The road is hard for a reason. It's meant to weed out those who aren't ready or don't really want it. What I love about this story isn't that I kept going and ultimately succeeded. It's that for three years straight, I was the one being weeded out. For three years straight, I walked a difficult path and was told, "You're not good enough." Every time I saw that rejection letter, I had to make a decision. Was I going to let this break my resolve—or would I keep going, whatever it takes, until I had earned it?

The Hard Road Versus the Easy Fix

The polar opposite of this story is the cautionary tale of the parents from the 2019 Operation Varsity Blues scandal who bought their kids' admissions to Ivy League schools through a conspiracy to bribe college coaches. These parents robbed their own kids of the opportunity to find honor and self-respect through hard work and delayed gratification.

When the Varsity Blues scandal was all over the news, I frequently found myself thinking back on my own college-admissions process. Ultimately, I got accepted, but it was the struggle to get there that made the difference in my life, not the acceptance. Hell, the degree didn't even matter. I earned a textiles degree that I barely used then and hardly use today (although I can probably still determine the time period of the fashion in any television show based solely on women's hemlines). The only thing that ended up mattering was the fight to reach my goal.

Maybe that's why I'm so irked by participation trophies. Self-esteem comes from the struggle it takes to improve enough to win, whatever "winning" means to you. For some, winning means coming in first; for others, it's improving your time or conquering an obstacle or finishing a 10K. But if you don't do something hard to get the external reward, "the trophy," victory loses its meaning.

When we talk about participation awards, we're almost always talking about kids. However, I'm more amazed at how regularly I'm faced with adults who have the "participation award" mindset. Don't believe me? Does any of this sound familiar?

- I worked a full day, so I deserve to watch a few hours of Netflix when I get home instead of engaging with my family or friends or working on a hobby that might help me grow into the person I want to be one day.
- I was super productive in that meeting, so I deserve to pick up Chick-fil-A on the way home instead of making myself a nutritious meal and investing in my health.
- I put in over forty hours of work this week, so I deserve to do nothing on the weekend except watch movies and sleep in.
- I ran a mile this morning, so I deserve that doughnut for breakfast.
- I did a Spartan race last year, so I don't need to do one this year. I don't need to try to beat my time for a personal best.

It doesn't matter what we use as justification—our workday, our morning workout, past accomplishments—it's the justification itself that is the problem.

Your mental justifications and rationalizations have the full force of a participation trophy. The justification of "I did this, so I get that" leads to a mindset of entitlement every time and is keeping you from true resilience. The most accomplished people I know, the ones with an abundance of true resilience, refuse to rest on their laurels. It doesn't even occur to them that they "earned" something because, the truth is, the struggle is the reward.

I've found that it's easier for me to practice this in my own life; when it comes to the people around me, it gets messier. Emotions are involved, and I don't like to see my colleagues or family members with hurt feelings or bruised egos. So how do we resist giving ourselves (or our kids, colleagues, friends, and family) a reward, large or small, for nothing? How do we encourage ourselves to delay gratification in favor of patience, commitment, and effort? How do we fight the immediate gratification that leads to entitlement, softness, and unhappiness? How do we make ourselves *earn* it?

Small acts of discipline and purposeful patience matter. They build character. To understand how this works, you first have to know something about pleasure as a motivator for human behavior. You have to start with something as small as a marshmallow.

The Pleasure Principle

Human beings instinctively seek pleasure (chocolate cake, video games, new gadgets, a soft couch) and avoid pain (homework, saving money, burpees). Sigmund Freud called it the "pleasure principle."

According to Freud's theory, when we were children, we were driven by the id, a primitive part of our personality that motivated us to seek immediate gratification to satisfy cravings like hunger and thirst and to avoid any discomfort. It's the reason infants cry for milk. It's also the reason kids stomp their feet when they want a new toy or whine for a Slurpee at 7-Eleven.

As we mature, we learn (or should learn) that delaying gratification yields greater rewards than caving to the immediate craving. But it's a tough skill to develop, especially if we become accustomed to getting what we want immediately, for little or no effort.

In a country of abundance, we don't have to wait for much anymore. We are conditioned by society to expect rewards without effort or struggle. "Unlimited lives" in a computer game, instant approval for credit cards and loans, special lines at the airport and theme parks where we pay extra to cut in front of others, fast-food restaurants and door-to-door delivery services, and, of course, participation trophies. Pleasure on demand is reinforced in the videos we watch, the music we listen to, and the advertising we see.

In research later dubbed the Stanford marshmallow experiment, Professor Walter Mischel explored instant and delayed gratification in preschoolers and how both choices impacted the children's future development. I like to think of the results of this experiment both in terms of the effects we might have on children now and the ways our own development as adults may have been misguided when we were growing up.

The rules for the first part of the study were straightforward. A number of preschoolers were offered a treat, such as a marshmallow or a pretzel stick. Each child was given the choice of eating one treat now or waiting fifteen minutes and receiving two treats. Only one in three children could delay their satisfaction by waiting for the second sweet.

The second part of the study monitored the participants over the course of the next thirty years as they grew from preschooler to teenager to adult. These follow-up sessions found a surprising correlation between the results of the original experiment and later success in life. The kids who had been unable to delay gratification—the ones who gobbled down the single marshmallow—had higher rates of drug abuse and addiction as adults, along with higher incarceration rates. The children who had been able to hold out for the better reward got higher grades in school, were physically healthier and less likely to be obese or have addictions, enjoyed greater professional achievements, and were more successful in relationships. The self-control they had shown as children had not dissipated as they matured, and that skill enabled them to make wise and deliberate decisions throughout their lives.

The general results of the experiment weren't necessarily a revelation. After all, patience is a virtue that has been celebrated through the ages. The Spartans honored patience. They trained their warriors for up to ten years before they went into battle. And as Benjamin Franklin accurately pointed out, "He that can have patience can have what he will." But the specific outcomes of the marshmallow experiment did get scientists and educators wondering whether the kids who could delay their gratification had a natural capacity for endurance-based success or whether patience was a trait that could be learned.

Over the last few decades, other researchers continued to explore impulse control. Mischel himself did a deeper dive, as well. Almost all of the studies came back with the same result: waiting is hard but can be learned. It's a matter of putting in the effort.

Now, this is really important, so I want to stop here for a second and let that sink in. Patience can be learned. Therefore, it follows that labels like *impatient* and *impulsive* and *reckless* need not apply to us for the entirety of our lives. It is within our power to train those qualities out of existence. It's harder, of course, when it comes to our kids because impulsivity is also dependent on brain growth and development. The prefrontal cortex, the decision-making center, isn't fully formed until around age twenty-five, so the younger you are, the less impulse control you have.

During our Kids Death Race last summer, I called Dr. L and asked, "How do I get these kids to stop complaining?" Her answer was simple: "You can't. They're going to complain because their brain wants out. That's normal. What you've got to do is intervene with the parents. Just because kids complain and impulsively want to escape doesn't mean the parents have to listen and fix it. Not every cry for help is a cry worth listening to. And this is how you help train patience—for both parent and child."

As adults, we know that the best payoffs usually emerge slowly and not very dramatically. It may help to recognize that delaying gratification is not just a means to an end. It's a tool. The kids who resisted the first marshmallow in Mischel's experiment didn't know that they were laying the foundation for remarkable inner strength. But the more you practice delaying gratification, the easier it will become.

How to Practice Delayed Gratification on Yourself

Maybe when you were growing up you were one of those kids who couldn't wait for the second marshmallow. Or maybe you could wait then, but you've unlearned some of that delayed gratification thanks to cell phones, one-click purchases, and the other "instant gratification" forces that dominate our lives. I get it. A lot of us grew up learning the wrong things, and then those bad habits were reinforced over and over again by parents, teachers, coaches, and mentors. Suddenly, we're adults with a warped way of thinking and living, and we can't quite figure out why things seem so tangled for us.

This warped thinking doesn't present itself as clearly as a marshmallow for adults. It shows up as people-pleasing and intolerance for uncertainty. I meet people all the time who show up at my farm to learn how to become more disciplined in exercise and fitness, only to realize that every other part of their life could use the same rigorous attention. Maybe you spend too much money on things you don't need and go into debt because of it. Maybe you have a hard time saying no to friends or bosses, even when the activity or assignment will be damaging.

The gift of the marshmallow experiment results isn't the realization that patience early in life leads to more success down the line; it's that patience itself can be learned. Remember in rule 1 when we talked about knocking down that decrepit old building in your mind so you can make room for a solid structure based on proven principles? Delayed gratification is like a single brick. Each time you delay gratification—in any aspect of your life—you are laying another brick for this new and better structure. Eventually, you'll have a life built on a solid foundation.

Here are some ways we can practice delaying gratification as adults:

- Waiting for others to finish talking before we jump in with our opinion
- Passing on the quick rush of a candy bar in favor of the slow burn of a healthy carbohydrate like a sweet potato
- Budgeting and tracking spending as opposed to blowing our paycheck the minute we get it
- Showing up for every training opportunity at work or beyond, even for things we "already know"

While it might seem like delaying gratification is about saying no, as in the marshmallow experiment, it's really about saying yes to the difficult path. When I ask those who come to me for help to think of it this way, it makes the concept easier. Instead of telling yourself, *No, I'm not going to grab that stale Halloween candy that's in a bowl on the counter*, you can say, *Yes, I'm going to take the path of waiting for dinner*. When you're faced with a difficult email or a troubling phone call, you can say no to a quick, defensive, and reactionary response, and yes to thinking about it for a beat and taking the time to respond appropriately. That's delayed gratification at work in your life in the best way.

Physicality

One of the best ways to build the kind of mental fortitude that allows you to delay gratification is to do something physical. Sadly, reading this book and others like it may help you understand the value of these skills, but you won't actually build resilience through reading. In my experience, you have to get into the arena and actually move your body in some physical way toward a goal.

Physicality makes accomplishment and progress easy to see and track. And it sets the stage for what delayed gratification really looks like. For example, if you've never run more than three miles, set a goal to run for six. Each week increase your mileage by just 10 percent. Don't do more than that. Be patient, trust the process. You'll see the progress. It might be painstakingly slow, but the end will be worth it when you see six miles pop up on your tracking device. Ever wonder why people quit their fitness goals so quickly? Because they think they can just jump into the game and hotwire their fitness from couch potato to clearing a marathon in just a few weeks. Not gonna happen. Want to do five hundred burpees in a day? You could try and power through—or you could start with fifty and add ten more every day. It may take you forty-five days, but the gradual increase will set the stage for that incredible celebration when you reach your goal.

You can use this model to develop any new skill or talent, like learning a language or playing a musical instrument. If you believe you can do it and you take action, you will see results. Now throw in some of the inevitable hardship, adversity, screwups, and setbacks that naturally occur along the way, and you will begin to develop the special sauce of the growth mindset: resilience.

Earned, Not Given:
For the Family

Charlie is our second son, a middle child, and, like all kids, he used to act up when he was little. Back when he was still in footie pajamas, Charlie was driving me crazy, not listening, in the run-up to Christmas. Like parents often do, I told him Santa might not bring presents if he didn't improve his behavior. Most parents say this and don't mean it, but I believe follow-through, discipline, and consequences are critical, even when it comes to Santa. I decided I couldn't just give him rewards without some hard work, but I didn't see a teachable moment in filling his stocking with coal, either. I believe that you've got to give kids a chance to show what they're made of.

So I decided I was going to set his presents on Tent Mountain, a one-thousand-foot hill behind our home in Vermont. I managed to get my wife, Courtney, to go along with it, perhaps because she's so tuned in to what motivates each of our kids. Let me pause here and say that leading like this is difficult. You have to enforce consequences; you have to make kids (or colleagues, teammates, etc.) work instead of setting a reward in front of them for no reason. You can't just hand them the iPad or chocolate when they have not earned it. In this case, my philosophy meant carting Charlie's presents up a one-thousand-foot hill in a Christmas Eve blizzard. It took me ninety minutes. On Christmas morning, the other three kids woke up to presents under the tree, and Charlie got nothing but a note from Santa. Charlie was a little disappointed when I told him Santa didn't want to make the effort to bring all his presents down the chimney because he hadn't been entirely good, but that he had set them on the peak to see if Charlie had the guts to go get them.

Charlie put his coat and boots on over his footie pajamas. He took my hand and made that climb. In the snow and wind, it became a quest we shared. When he found his presents covered with a dusting of snow on the peak, my son smiled and got a look in his eyes I'll never forget. It was pretty magical to see how proud he felt. Those presents meant a thousand times more to him than anything Santa could have set under the tree, because Charlie had worked to get them. He'd earned them.

HOW TO PRACTICE DELAYED GRATIFICATION WITH YOUR KIDS

If you teach delayed gratification early—maybe with some marshmallows or Christmas presents—your kids will someday appreciate living by its truth. A sports analogy is a good way to consider the art of delayed gratification. Let's say your daughter is learning to hit a softball. The more she practices her swing, and the more she practices laying off bad pitches, the more singles, doubles, triples, and home runs she's likely to hit over time. Every time she lets a bad pitch sail on by and waits for something better, she strengthens her resolve to resist short-term temptations. She learns to pause before acting on impulse and to ask herself, *How important is it that I have this right now?*

Like any life skill, delayed gratification and hard work can be learned. Delayed gratification is like a superpower for those of us who can manage it. As adults, things frequently don't go our way. We don't always get what we want. We won't always get into our first-choice school on the first try, and that's part of our journey. The same will one day be true for your kids. So teach them early that the thing they actually want will take patience, effort, and endurance. Everything in your life that matters is earned, not given. Then watch as they get the blessing of two marshmallows instead of one throughout their life.

Here are some practical ways to introduce the practice of delayed gratification to kids:

- Give your child a multi-action goal, something to work up to over time, for a solid reward. For example, doing one chore doesn't unlock the $5 weekly allowance; only completing a whole week of chores finalizes the exchange.
- Your child wants a specific toy? Great. Tell him, "You can have that toy in one month if you make your bed every day, keep your room tidy, and clean the guinea pig cage once a week. If you do that for a total of thirty days, we'll get you that toy."
- Purposefully bring your child into the toy section of a department store and browse the aisles. Allow her to identify something she wants "in the future." Then leave without getting anything. Tell her she has to think of a reward system to earn

the toy. Invite her to come up with the task and the deadline, which you'll approve.

- Teach your kids the difference between "want" and "need," and make them be specific in their language when they ask for something. For example, if they say, "I *need* those Pokémon cards," say, "No, you *want* those Pokémon cards." Explain that needs are things like water, food, and shelter and that wants come from a different motivation.

- Use the "marble jar method" as a visual way for your children to see progress toward their goal. Have your kid identify something they want (like a baseball glove or a Lego set or a chemistry kit), and tape a picture of that item to the jar as a reminder of the reward. Then identify ways in which the child can accumulate marbles to fill the jar—like one marble each time they show good behavior in the grocery store, use good manners at the table, or eat all their vegetables. Each time they receive another marble, have them drop it in the jar themselves so they can monitor their progress toward their reward.

- Go for a long hike or bike ride or some other prolonged activity that requires you to stop along the way to rest. At each pit stop, take stock of how far you have come and how much farther it will be until you get where you are going. Use this as a way to illustrate that, like hiking to the summit of Tent Mountain, any worthwhile goal takes many steps, and the effort makes reaching the goal that much sweeter. When the goal is attained, take time to remember and celebrate each of the steps along the way.

Challenging your kids to do difficult, uncomfortable things is another way to illustrate how capable they are of holding off instant pleasure or comfort. This is the power of manufactured adversity. It's a way to practice tolerating what's hard in a controlled manner. One key is to make each manufactured challenge a game. Here are some examples:

- Challenge older kids to try cold showers for three days to see how great a hot shower feels on the fourth day.
- Challenge teens to do without television for two weeks, and reward them with tickets to a big movie or concert of their choice.
- Challenge your kids to hold a plank pose for thirty to sixty seconds before dinner. Better yet, get the whole family involved. Whoever caves first has to do the dinner dishes.
- Your kid wants a new video game? Say, "Okay, but only after you read five books in five weeks."
- For the littlest kids, you can do this, too—just make sure you're choosing something that their growing brains can latch on to. See who can hold their breath the longest each time you drive through a tunnel. Challenge them not to touch any toys for five minutes as they walk through a store. Invite them to leave their favorite doll downstairs for twenty minutes before bedtime. The reward does not have to be material; teach them that

their feeling of accomplishment is something special in and of itself.

Courtney once challenged our kids to read one hundred books in thirty days. She loves reading and had always hoped that her kids would enjoy reading as well. They were younger and so they counted every book—even the small board books. When one of the kids finished a book, they were allowed to take a big marker and write the name of the book on a poster. They got extra points when the bigger kids read to the little ones. They accomplished the feat and weren't even interested in the reward. It was all about the process and having fun!

WHEN THINGS GET TOUGH . . .

No one enjoys being sad, disappointed, angry, tense, stressed, scared, or uncomfortable, but these feelings are a normal part of life. They're a critical part of what makes us human. It's important to accept the many lessons of difficult emotions in the journey of life and not pander to your children when they express distress as they take small steps toward their goals.

Too often, parents try to protect their children from difficult emotions. They are uncomfortable when their children feel sad or stressed or angry, and they do everything in their power to sweep the most painful emotions under the rug. They coddle their kids when intense feelings are present. They soothe and pacify the moment there is any pain, offer up ice cream after a soccer game loss, give in to tantrums, change the subject when it turns gloomy. "Let's be happy!" they demand from the driver's seat of the minivan. This is a costly practice. It creates kids who can't handle perfectly normal feelings, setbacks, and disappointments. One of the essential parts of practicing delayed gratification is built into the term—*delay* the gratification. If your children are complaining or whining and you pacify them, the foundation on which they were building the skill is wiped clean.

Parents also need to watch how they handle their own struggle with delayed gratification and the hard feelings that come with it. If you constantly try to avoid your own uncomfortable emotions, your kids will learn to do the same. Remember, you have to build this inside of you and model it for your kids. If you've set a goal for yourself but cave when things get hard, so will they. Instead, teach your kids to embrace the suck and work through it. You can do this by addressing your kids' painful feelings head-on and by dealing with them out in the open. No sugarcoating. No giving in. No gift wrapping. It may be a more laborious, intense way of parenting, but if your children do not learn to deal with adversity and unwanted emotions, they have almost no chance of growing into emotionally healthy adults.

In Conclusion

Think about some of your greatest accomplishments in life—owning a home, being debt free, building your own company, climbing the corporate ladder, having a healthy relationship with your spouse or your kids. I bet whatever you chose, the accomplishment was earned. You worked toward this accomplishment with grit, perseverance, and commitment. Sure, you probably fucked up along the way, but you kept going. You knew that the reward at the end was going to be worth it, and that's what allowed you to keep moving no matter how hard it was. On our Spartan Kids finisher T-shirt is the phrase EARNED, NOT GIVEN, and we mean it. We aren't a trophy culture company, and I'll never be a trophy culture dad. The hard work, the delayed gratification, the "I finally did it!" feeling—they're all part of the recipe of resilience. And let's be clear, the hard work is *hard*. That's the point. Even as you read this book, you'll encounter parts that will make you squirm or want to put the book down. That's the point. Hard work equals growth.

Keep in mind that as you begin to implement some of the strategies and tools in this book, you will need to practice the very thing that I'm teaching you now: delayed gratification. You may see glimmers of progress along the way, but your kids aren't going to turn into superstars overnight, and you're certainly not going to transform into a superhero parent with the snap of your fingers. Saddle up for a long, grueling ride. And don't cave or quit. When all is said and done, you'll be glad you took the hard steps—even if your kids don't thank you until they're thirty.

Commit to No Bullshit

Eliminate the Excess and the Excuses

> An excuse is more terrible and worse than a lie; for an excuse is a guarded lie.
>
> —Alexander Pope

There is no greater threat to true resilience than your own bullshit. It's vital that you start to recognize your excuses, mental blocks, and bad habits so that when they appear, you know how to toss them aside. If you continually give in to your bullshit, nurturing and protecting the parts of you that are holding you back, you'll never have the breakthroughs, wins, and satisfactions that lead to true resilience.

I get many emails every day that read something like this: I quit drinking. I lost one hundred pounds. I fixed my marriage. I started my own company.

I don't tell you this to gloat. Those emails aren't invigorating to me because they make me feel proud; they are exciting because they remind me that change is real. Transformations are happening in people's lives all over the world.

However, sometimes it's hard not to think about the other side of that coin: all the people who woke up this morning and did the same bullshit behaviors that have them stuck in a rut. I fear that stagnation is more the norm than transformation. It's why I'm so committed to the mission of Spartan. I've seen the kinds of transformations in others that make it very easy for me to say to you now: if they can do it, so can you.

You Need Data

When people come to Spartan wanting to run a race or change their life, I start by reminding them that no one ever "changed" anything in their life by sitting on the couch eating popcorn and watching Netflix. You're not going to suddenly have a lightning-bolt moment and change. I'm not saying lightning-bolt moments never occur. (Remember the kid who biked with me to Vermont? He certainly had one.) But, in my experience, they're not common.

Not a lot changes in your life if you're still indulging your bullshit. So how *do* people change? First, you do what you read about in chapter 1 on limitations: you start noticing the thought patterns that are holding you back, and you try to redirect those limiting narratives to growth narratives. Next, you let some kind of challenge inspire and motivate you, and without those limitations, you allow yourself to say yes, sign up, and go for it. After that, be prepared to be scared out of your mind. There's no backing away from the challenge now.

Let's take Spartan races, for example. Imagine that a newcomer arrives to do his first Spartan obstacle course race. The race might involve running a 5K on difficult terrain, crawling in the mud, doing a rope climb or a spear throw, clambering over military walls, or carrying sandbags. He has never done any of this before. While it might look like he is unprepared and out of his element, that's an important place to be. Running your first obstacle race isn't just something hard you're doing; it's the first step on the path of transformation.

The newcomer is getting a visceral and intense look at exactly where he is and exactly where he wants to go. He is being told for the first time in his life to jump into the mud—not walk around it, but get into it. This blows his mind. For his entire life, he was told not to get dirty. But the nine thousand other people on the course seem unafraid. Those nine thousand other people just helped our newcomer see a new possibility. The newcomer arrived with some mental bullshit, and in just one day on an obstacle course that he was wildly unprepared for, he has successfully learned something about himself that will serve him in the future. He has created an RDP—a resilience data point.

If you're sitting on the couch watching Netflix, you have no idea how many miles you can run or if you can learn how to play that song on the piano or write a chapter of a book. You have no data. Where are you on the long and arduous road to achieving your goals? Most people have no idea because they are opting out of the journey alto-gether. Worse yet, consider the data that your children have for feeling resilient and confident because of a previous challenge. Oh, they don't have any data? That's a problem. We need more of these data points in our lives, and our kids do, too. We need more moments that we can call up to remind us that we are more capable than our bullshit tells us.

Beware of Your Own Bullshit

Whenever I work out with someone who is coming to the gym for the first time or returning after spending a few years (or decades!) not working out, one thing happens without fail: that person typically arrives for the first day in brand-new workout clothes, looking like a human Nike advertisement. They will literally be ripping the price tags off their new REI or Lululemon gear as they walk in the door. They will have a high-tech water bottle and clean shoes. They will think they've come "prepared" and "ready for anything," but do you know what I see when I look at all that stuff? Yep. I see bullshit.

The stuff you buy does not define you. I see it all the time, a faulty investment in gear because some people believe it will help them achieve their goals faster, when in reality it's principles like commitment, hard work, and accountability that get you across the finish line. This is one of the first obstacles you need to confront on a path to resilience. Looking the part does not make you the part. You're trying to expedite progress without doing the work, and it's bullshit.

Maybe this will sound familiar: You decide to try something new, reach a goal you've had for a while, and because of your fears and insecurities—that you might fail, might not be any good, won't achieve anything, or imagine someone will laugh at you when you show up looking clueless—you make a beeline for the mall or Amazon. Whether you realize it or not, you're trying to cover yourself in the *image* of what you want to be before you've done the work to actually become that person. Maybe you've always dreamed of being a famous painter. However, because you're afraid of the discomfort you might feel as you attempt to learn this new skill, you spend an inordinate amount of time researching oils and pastels and brushes. Eventually, you buy enough paint and brushes and easels for an army of painters, then hit the couch and turn on Netflix, never to paint again!

Why do we do this? Our bullshit is the stuff we intentionally put between our current unsatisfying and overly comfortable life and the fulfilling and uncomfortable life we want. Excuses, high expectations, pursuit of perfection—we plant them right in the gap between where we are and where we want to be, and we give them permission to block us. Let me free you of that bullshit once and for all. You don't need a new pair of tennis shoes to start doing burpees today and continue every day for the rest of your life. Heck, do them barefoot in the grass in your underwear for all I care. You don't even need a dumbbell to start doing bicep curls—grab a book or a bottle of water and *do it*. You don't need a new laptop to write a book. You don't need the latest and greatest painting supplies to learn to paint. When the urge creeps in to replace the real work with the bullshit stuff, notice it. And then call yourself up to live your life bullshit-free. This is the necessary next step to finding true resilience. You cannot weather tough storms in life if your bullshit is running the show.

The women in my family are some of the toughest people I've ever known. My wife, Courtney, who was a top soccer player in college, is one of the most disciplined, truth-telling, and persevering people in every room. Courtney calls me on my bullshit literally every single day. She is such a positive person. That's her superpower. She makes me laugh, keeps me grounded, and brings me back to earth when I float up into Joe land. I wouldn't be half as resilient as I am today without her influence. She is one of my biggest motivators in writing this book.

But I truly, *truly* learned how to recognize and discard my bullshit from my mother, Jean De Sena. She was so committed to living a no-bullshit life that she might as well have trademarked the title of this chapter. She knew herself, did what she thought was right, and was stunningly immune to trends.

Let me set the scene for you. It's the 1970s in Queens, New York. I'm a kid growing up in Howard Beach, a neighborhood full of wiseguys, where indulgence and overconsumption—drinking, smoking, and elaborate meals—are a way of life. (Ravioli for dinner. Cannoli for dessert. Not a fruit or a vegetable in sight.) My sister and I are with my mom and her sister, Mary Ellen, in Charles Memorial Park, near Kennedy Airport. There's a stench in the air from the nearby garbage dump, but the sun is glistening on the water, and I can see Mom and Aunt Mary Ellen running in silhouette. They run repeated loops around that park, over and over. I can still see them smiling, increasing their pace as they pass by a Nathan's hotdog seller. Eventually, they hit ten miles and stop.

I guess this wouldn't be a big deal today, but back then, nobody in my neighborhood ran unless they were being chased. Nobody worked out, did yoga, sought out health food, or became a vegan, but my mom had a mind of her own and a will made of solid iron. My mother's unfailing confidence and conviction, along with her willingness to stay open to new information and experiences, allowed her to learn and grow every day of her life. She was fiercely independent, undeniably brave, and always, without question, herself. As a parent, she modeled these qualities for my sister and me every day and instilled in us the desire to be just as strong, just as open, and just as tough. She realized we needed that grit to make our way in the world.

My mother knew that life outside our house—and sometimes *inside* our house—wasn't easy. For most of my childhood, we lived in a rough Italian neighborhood. (If you've seen the movie *Goodfellas*, well, that was Mayberry by comparison.) Several people in our family were locked up for committing stupid crimes. My workaholic father and my tough-as-nails mother would often get into actual fistfights at home.

My parents were, in many ways, oil and water. Dad was always looking for his next business venture; Mom couldn't have cared less about money. He would bring home junk food and other treats to make up for being late; she was 100 percent focused on health and wellness and made sure we practiced healthy habits.

But my mom wasn't always this way. When I was very young, my mom was just like everyone else in our neighborhood, eating pasta and processed food and staying sedentary most of the day. Then her mom died from cancer. It lit a fire under her to figure out how she could improve her body and mind. In her quest for better health, Mom found the one natural foods store in our neighborhood amid all the Italian restaurants and corner bodegas. There she met Swami Bua, an Indian yogi who had moved to New York City to teach. After hearing his story, she not only tried yoga and meditation but fully embraced a healthy lifestyle. And she began to instill the same passion for health and exercise in my sister and me. She even wound up introducing friends in our community to the world's longest footrace (which she also ran in), the Self-Transcendence 3,100-mile race established by Sri Chinmoy, in which athletes run a single loop again and again in what becomes like a meditative chant of a run, around and around.

Of course, it wasn't easy to make healthy choices in our community. It took grit and ingenuity to both discover and maintain a consistent practice of self-care. Our neighbors didn't understand why Mom would rather do sun salutations or run laps than gossip over a glass of wine. After my parents divorced, my mother moved us to a small town in upstate New York. We landed down the street from Cornell University, an Ivy League school in Ithaca. Her goal was to build a better life. Not only was Mom trying to find a safer neighborhood and a better education for her kids, but she wanted us to live in a community that shared her healthy values.

We didn't know a soul in our new town, and from that emerged some of the most uncomfortable moments of my life. And it wasn't just me—my mom and my sister were equally as unsteady in that new setting. We were all forced to step out of our comfort zones. I was thirteen at the time, so it wasn't easy leaving friends and family behind. If you've relocated while your kids were still in school, you know how tough it can be.

But here's where the lesson of this chapter comes into full force, and why committing to no bullshit is the first step to resilience. After the move, Mom continued to push herself. Here she was, a single mother of two teenagers. She had just uprooted herself, separated herself from everything she had ever known, and forced her kids to do the same. We were uncomfortable making new friends, finding a new lifestyle, learning the rules of a new place. Mom didn't miss a beat. She didn't need a new haircut or everyone to like her to accomplish what she wanted to accomplish in this new place. Almost immediately, she was practicing yoga, running, and visiting health food stores. She dove deeper into her meditative lifestyle and became a full-blown yogi, even traveling to India alone to explore the practice. She didn't speak any of the languages in India, but as you can now imagine, that didn't hold her back.

Now that I'm a parent and an adult, I can say for certain that she was scared at times. The struggles of day-to-day life probably threatened to distract her from what she was working toward. If it was hard for me or my sister to make new friends, would she let that be an excuse to move us back to Queens? What if she missed her own friends or family? What if she had a distracted or frustrating day with her meditation practice or sustained an injury during one of her long runs? Would that be the thing that let her take the more comfortable, established path in life?

Instead of nurturing her bullshit, Mom nurtured her desire to build resilience in herself and others. And that's the thing—a no-bullshit person isn't someone who is fearless. A no-bullshit person knows the value of facing fears head-on. Jean De Sena was someone who was true to her own values, confident in herself, and capable of facing anything the world threw at her. She was truly resilient. And I became more resilient from experiencing the world alongside her.

Choose Your Own Adventure

The extreme yogic lifestyle my mom chose halfway through her life left an impression on me and is probably the key reason I believed I could start and lead my own company. In so many ways, she is the essence of Spartan. There was nothing fancy about her; she just wanted better. She practiced discipline and was disrupting the system before the system even knew it was broken. She didn't let the critics, the masses, perfection, or expectations get in her way.

When I launched Spartan in 2010, the fitness and health industries were focused on shortcuts and instant fixes. Magazines promised abs in seven minutes, and videos proclaimed that you could be a champion with only negligible effort. It was all a bit ridiculous. I remembered what my mom taught me, that it was up to me to create my own path. No one was going to do it for me, and if I caved to the critics, I would end up miserable. True to form, your own path is most likely going to be the most difficult one. It's easy to conform. It's easy to play the part and talk the talk. It's not as easy to walk where you want and confront the bullshit that's on your route—even if it's your own. My mom's way of being and doing has been the guiding light of my company from the beginning.

Commit to No Bullshit: For the Family

It's really important to give the gift of no bullshit to other people, especially your kids. Nowadays there's even more bullshit that can interrupt your own kids' paths toward resilience. Whether it's social media, a "keeping up with the Joneses" mentality, or the pursuit of perfection, we have our work cut out for us when it comes to bagging the BS. Here are some lessons for doing just that.

KNOW YOURSELF, AND BE TRUE TO YOURSELF

What can you learn from Jean De Sena? First and foremost, get to know yourself and get to know your kids. You can't recognize your bullshit if you don't know what it looks like. One way it can show up is by trying to mask who you really are. Many people care way too much about what other people are doing and how they stack up in the community. My mom never cared if people thought she was odd. It simply didn't matter to her. She worked hard to discover what she believed in, she figured out what was most important to her, and she embraced alternative lifestyle choices like yoga and veganism well before most people had heard of either, much less understood their health benefits. The key to this kind of confidence is truly understanding yourself and being true to your values. Ask yourself where you might be sacrificing what matters because you're worried about how you might be perceived. And tune in to your own kids to notice if they may be doing the same. If your daughter loves her violin but all of a sudden stores it in her closet because it's "not something the popular kids do," talk to her about it and remind her that she can't please everyone. Work hard to show your kids that being true to yourself is a key part of developing a healthy relationship with yourself.

KINDNESS BREEDS KINDNESS, AND BULLSHIT BREEDS BULLSHIT

There are approximately 4,200 religions in the world. While the details of each may vary, the big themes remain the same in almost all of those belief systems. Be kind. Help others. Do good. Whether you are religious, atheist, or agnostic, focus your energy on treating all people with respect and dignity. When you exercise your bullshit outward toward other people—whether it's through obvious disrespect or underground bullying—that stuff only comes back to bite you in the end. Dr. L says, "Hate is like a boomerang. When you spew hate toward others, it comes back around and creates a deep sense of self-loathing. It can be an enormous barrier to change and growth." My mother accepted everyone she met for who they were, and I believe in doing the same. Modeling that attitude and behavior for your kids is one of the greatest gifts you can give them. Don't tolerate it when they say unkind things about peers or even strangers, for that matter. Be aware of the kind of language you use to describe other people, and set guidelines for what's acceptable in the family and what's not. You don't have to like everyone, but you should respect them and demonstrate that attitude of respect in front of your children at all times. My mom always said, "When in doubt, close your mouth." I try to remember to consciously self-edit and to be especially careful to keep my mouth shut when strong emotions take hold. Before I speak, I take a deep breath and consider the possible impact of my words. Haven't we all regretted something we've said in anger? Let's learn from that experience.

MODEL IMPERFECTION

The pursuit of perfection may be one of the biggest bullshit creators. So many people get caught up in the idea that "if it's not perfect, I'm not doing it." They don't see that their own desire for unwavering perfection is keeping them stuck. Dr. L informed me that perfectionism and procrastination are highly correlated. I didn't believe her at first. I thought that if someone is trying to be perfect, they'll do whatever it takes to get their shit done. But after considering Dr. L's point, I agree that it makes complete sense. The pursuit of perfection actually prevents people from getting anything done because they are so hell-bent on making sure their work is free of any flaw. My mom was the first to acknowledge her imperfections and admit when she made a mistake in every area of her life. She didn't try to hide her failures from me or my sister. This is key to leading your kids to be at least as resilient as you hope to be. When we fail in front of our children, it is important to verbally recognize and admit to that mistake right away. Circle back and let them know you've made a mistake. Taking responsibility in front of your kids matters. They'll be more honest and resilient about their own mistakes if you are with yours. When they fail, celebrate it. Explain the concept of failing forward, learning from mistakes, and the wisdom you gain from being imperfect. Don't slap just your children's A+ tests on the fridge. Put the C– ones up there as well, and ask them to write on a sticky note what they learned so it becomes a frame of reference for the ebbs and flows of success.

GRATITUDE, NOT GREED

My sister and I used to whine over who had more food on our plate. My mom would look at us and say, "You get what you get, and don't get upset." It's not like we were going to starve. We both had full plates in front of us—something many children are not privileged enough to have—and we should have known to be grateful. We were always fed and clothed and had a roof over our heads. Mom helped us understand how fortunate we were. Comparison can rob you of any gains you feel like you're making. The bullshit comparative games that we sometimes play prevent us from moving forward and making moves. "I'll never get as far as he did," we say. Or "I'll never be as successful as she is." It's killing our mojo, and it will kill your kids' mojo, too. In our land of relative comfort and abundance, we need to help our children understand the value of what is present in their lives and not focus on what they wish they had. Want more resilient kids? Teach them the practice of gratitude. It's the gateway to a healthier attitude. Be a family that says thanks, no matter what's on the plate. Have your kids name three things that they are grateful for over breakfast—one person, one place, and one thing. It's a simple game that can breed a lifetime of gratitude.

INCONSISTENCY IS YOUR BULLSHIT

Time after time I see parents struggle with inconsistency, which is a huge problem in parenting. They set rules, then break them. They promise, then fail to follow through. They say yes, then later say no. They say no, then later cave in. Extreme flexibility may be the easiest path in the moment: quickly shifting from no to yes, or bending a rule just so the nagging stops. I get it. I've been there. But pervasive inconsistencies erode the trust you are building with your children and can create anxiety at a very young age.

Unfortunately, when we are tired, we tend toward inconsistency. We loosen the reins on our rules, or we say yes to something when we usually say no. But your child needs to know that you will respond with consistency in common situations. They desperately need to feel the security of the boundaries you set. Over time, they begin to internalize and build a blueprint for how you connect, how you discipline, and how you create a sense of structure. When you become inconsistent, their blueprint falls apart, and this unpredictability feels unsafe.

Consistency also helps kids organize the world, which creates additional safety. Do your best to be as consistent as possible with how you respond to everyday situations, how you enforce the rules that you set, and how you communicate the expectations that you hold. Of course, there are times when things go off course—and sometimes those can be excellent learning moments for both you and your kids—but try to be as consistent as possible.

I asked hundreds of people I admire to share the most important lesson they learned for success. Here are my favorites:

- When you have a choice between hard and easy, choose hard.
- If someone hands you something, you don't want it.
- Nothing in life is easy; working hard is crucial to survival.
- Respect powerful and dangerous things, but don't fear them.
- When you go to a job interview, always be polite to the receptionist.
- Our greatest griefs are those we create ourselves.
- You can't get better by practicing against someone who is worse than you.
- No matter what others do, keep doing the right thing, and you'll come out ahead.

In Conclusion

We've all got our bullshit that stands in the way of our greatest, most resilient self. After reading through this chapter, I hope you have a sense of what yours might be. Making excuses? Taking shortcuts when you haven't done the work? Being inconsistent? Caring more about what others think? Whatever it is, don't let yourself off the hook by just knowing it. Instead, do something about it. Think of bullshit like weeds in the garden. You can't just clip the top off the weed. You've got to remove the roots—get in there and pull it all out. This can require some deep digging.

I think that one of our greatest obstacles in life is the stories we tell ourselves. There's an excuse available to us at every turn, and if we turn those excuses into fully fleshed-out stories about what we are capable of, then we'll never collect the data we need to build resilience. We have to be the hero of our own story, not the boring character. I've learned over time with Spartan that it's not just the tough experience that draws people in; it's the story they get to tell afterward. They emerged as the heroes, the ones who overcame the obstacles—not the ones who quit because they didn't have the right gear, the proper fuel, or the right GPS watch. The pride and celebration that they get to share with others are equally as important. You won't be able to share a good, solid, honest story if you keep your life boring and you keep yourself weighed down with bullshit excuses for why you didn't do this or couldn't do that. One of the reasons that my mom was such a beast is because she owned all of her wild and wonderful parts. She kept herself and her life interesting—even with simple things like yoga and plants. You don't need to climb Everest to be a warrior—you just need to conquer your own excuses and teach your kids to do the same. Quit complaining, do the work, and get after it. It'll be worth it in the end because you'll be less inclined to get stuck, and so will your kids.

Live Your Values

Find Your True North and Communicate It

> You, who are on the road,
> Must have a code
> That you can live by.

—Crosby, Stills & Nash, "Teach Your Children"

When I was still building Spartan and organizing Spartan races, a company called Tough Mudder came out and became our direct and most punishing competition. Their obstacle course race itself was far less competitive than ours (that's my very biased opinion), but they had engaging branding that was connecting with people. Everything they did was written in bright orange letters, and their promotional videos featured a lot of high-fiving and smiling. Man, I hated them. Their marketing department had figured something out: how to make an obstacle course race feel like a social event instead of a challenge. And it worked.

The rules over at Tough Mudder events were different from ours. They allowed their athletes to skip obstacles while running the race—we enforced completion and added burpees when you couldn't master an obstacle. They gave participants headbands and a beer even if they hadn't done the full course. To me, that was maddening. There were athletes running those Tough Mudder races who had trained and trained, and they were crossing the finish line with someone who just showed up and took some selfies and barely broke a sweat. But there was something about the events that people enjoyed—the carefree fun, the camaraderie instead of competition, the crazy obstacles—Tough Mudder had found its audience.

As Tough Mudder started to take part of my business, I began to look at Spartan and feel really discouraged. My competitive nature flared up, and I got distracted by their different appeal. I felt like I was losing the battle of Spartan versus Tough Mudder. Year after year, the Tough Mudder races were called "creative" and "fun" and "team-based," and Spartan was referred to (accurately) as "physically challenging" and "every-man-for-himself." Logically, I understood that there were customers that were a better fit for Tough Mudder and those that were more inclined to come race with us, but when their races began filling up, I began to get nervous. Suddenly, I was faced with a decision: change what we were doing at Spartan or stay the course.

If you read the introduction of this book, you know that ultimately we won that competition. Spartan bought Tough Mudder, and we've brought them into our fold. I couldn't be more proud, as the incredible acquisition has allowed us to reach more customers, appeal to more personality types, and expand what we thought we knew about obstacle racing. But when we were down, a lot of people thought I should quit; they encouraged me to sell my company and get out while I still could. What no one understood, though, is that even as I was dazzled by the orange letters and the beer cans at the finish line, it didn't matter. I knew myself, and I knew my company. We had our priorities straight. We knew what we came to do. It's much easier to face adversity head-on when you've defined your priorities and have a sense of integrity.

More than ten million men and women have run Spartan races. Why? Spartan teaches people discipline, grit, and resilience. Spartan builds courage, composure, and confidence. Spartan gives participants an arena to practice the greatness that they rarely get to express—or maybe to explore the greatness they didn't know they have. If I undid the principles we were founded on, what would Spartan stand for?

My family wasn't exactly the sort that inherited a coat of arms. Yet the idea of a family crest, especially the motto, has always appealed to me. I liked the sense of direction and belonging that a motto can provide, like a north star to guide you when you get off course or face difficult decisions.

There were plenty of times I almost veered off course when I was young. My parents were constantly at odds, and I had to pick through pieces of their very different worldviews as I made my way. Maybe working so hard was what saved me. Long before I ever dreamed of Spartan, I established a multimillion-dollar pool and construction business as a teenager, sold it, and created a Wall Street trading firm. When I was young, I was always working, doing, hustling, and moving, and maybe that's why I really didn't examine my values until later in life. But when we began to build Spartan in 2009, it made me think about what I really believed in, the road map for living I wanted to share with the world. I got input from my Spartan team and began to understand how powerful it can be when people, within a company or a family, have clear goals, shared values, and a deep connection to both.

My business is driven by a shared belief system. Our mission is to transform one hundred million lives, and our belief system is that we *can*. We all need a true north, a vision statement that is grounded in a set of values and principles that you choose to guide your decisions. If we don't have one, we can fall out of line easily. Dr. L sees this time and time again in her practice, where clients either don't know their values at all or behave in a way that isn't in line with their values. "The bigger the gap between your values, your true north, and your behaviors, the greater the dis-ease," she says. "This dis-ease can come in the form of addiction, mental illness, general disinterest in life's journey, unhealthy relationships, or actual physical disease. We have to identify our values, and then we have to align our behaviors with them. This creates a congruence with what you believe and how you act. It grows integrity. If you are in alignment with your values, it's hard to go wrong. They become the guiding light for everything."

When I think of my own true north and the mission of Spartan, I realize that every decision I made is referenced to that value statement. Will this move the needle on transforming lives? Will this create greater opportunity to transform lives? Will this get us one step close to that one hundred million mark? When I use our value system as a guiding light for whether to move forward with something, I am honoring why we are here in the first place. It's not always easy. There are times when I have to turn away from a sponsor that is offering big bucks because their brand doesn't actually fit with our mission, but at least I'm operating with integrity.

I extend this concept into my family, with my wife and our kids. I knew that my family's true north would need to be a reflection of the collaborative way Courtney and I raise our children. What I have learned as a parent of four is that you can't really control how smart your kids are, how big they are, how athletically gifted they are, or even their temperaments. But you can influence how hard they work and how they see themselves and the world. Hard work will forge their characters. Hard work took me from a scrappy pool boy in Queens to the owner of the world's biggest obstacle course race empire. So the guiding light in my life and parenting became clear to me: *work hard.*

Courtney and I have similar values but different priorities. She'll tell you that I'm driven by accomplishment while she's more focused on our family's emotional well-being. I ask, "What did we all do today to make the world a better place?" She asks, "Are we content? Do we have close friends and good relationships?" Kindness is a priority for her, and I'm lucky as hell to have her as my partner. So it was important that we worked together and involved the kids when we came up with our family's vision statement. Here is what we came up with as a team. It's simple but it works:

"Work Hard. Be Nice."

Finding our true north was simple and incredibly meaningful for my family. Teamwork was central in Courtney's family—they weren't allowed to say, "I hate you," and her parents stressed the importance of being there for one another. So even the act of coming together as a family to do this activity was a demonstration of our allegiance to our values. Having a vision statement is necessary for acting on a goal. If you don't have a family yet, create a vision statement for yourself. If you want to set one for your team at work, there's no time like the present.

It's the Little Things
Courtney De Sena

My father worked for the FBI. I know—it was exciting and sounds cool in theory, but in practice it was hard at times on my family. He was a pilot who often traveled, and he couldn't always tell us where he was going. He'd sometimes show up to my soccer games or school concerts with a gun on his ankle holster and the stresses of his job looming. He loved his work and did his best to navigate the demands of his service with what was needed to be a present father. There was always an understanding that there would be times when his job would pull him away from us, and my mother was strong in keeping our family humming along while Dad was working on a case. We made sure to make the time we had with him as special as possible. And for us it was during family dinners when this time was best cultivated.

Hands down, the best memories of my childhood are sitting around laughing and talking at dinnertime. My parents and siblings all sat around our kitchen table, and a simple thirty-minute meal would turn into a long night. My parents have been married fifty-two years and have been an incredible example of unconditional love and how people don't need to be identical to make a marriage work. My mom is an artist and my dad is a military guy. They laugh and say that they have canceled each other out in every American presidential vote their whole married life. And while they are both unique people with different interests, their values are the same. They believe in a strong foundation of family. They love to have fun, and the dinner table was where we found our connectedness. We'd hear about Dad's travels and adventures, recount our weekly school happenings, play card games, and just tell stories. My father was the best storyteller, providing the smallest details that would draw us in and make us feel like we were there with him. My mom loved to tell stories about them being high school and college sweethearts and all their shared history. We loved hearing about our grandparents and their lives. While most kids can't wait to get up from the table and bound up the stairs to their own rooms, we didn't want to leave. The feeling of togetherness, joy, and pure belonging kept us glued to our chairs. This time was invaluable, especially as we understood that Dad's job could take him away on an assignment at a moment's notice. It was in these moments that I began to understand the value of small gestures and time.

When Joe and I started our own family and I thought about what I wanted our life to look like, my focus was clear: the little things. I didn't need or want extraordinary vacations, an extravagant home to raise the family in, or a playroom filled with all the coolest toys. I wanted *time* with my family. I wanted special moments, laughter, and stories. I wanted these little things, which I've learned actually become the big things. I want to know my kids and their friends and hear about their adventures and share our history. Ironically, I married a man who travels even more than my own father. So time and small moments matter a ton to our family. We are grateful for any time that the six of us can be together, no matter where we are—driving from one activity to the next, exercising together in the morning, or sitting at the dinner table after a long, hard day. It's these little things that matter most. I love watching Joe tell a story—he is charming and funny and lights up the room. And I love watching his face as our kids tell their stories. It's tucking the kids into their beds and taking the moment to lie down next to them and ask them about the day. It really is the little things.

Personal True North Exercise

Step 1

Begin by thinking about your truest self. What are your core values, the rock-solid things that matter most to you in the world? Consider the following:

Self-awareness
Perseverance
Passion
Discipline
Prioritizing
Grit
Courage
Optimism
Integrity
Wholeness

Ask yourself, *Do any of these virtues align with my personal values?* Are there other values that are not listed above that belong on your personal list? How about:

Kindness
Professionalism
Generosity
Compassion
Versatility
Independence
Decisiveness
Curiosity

Stability
Reliability
Loyalty
Service
Boldness
Honesty
Creativity
Toughness
Positivity
Faith

Another way to approach this exercise is to think about what matters most to you. Do any of these ideas resonate?

Being resilient
Being strong
Being honest
Being self-sufficient
Being wealthy and comfortable
Having a powerful job
Having social status
Having a healthy lifestyle
Spending time with family
Being compassionate
Being well educated
Being spiritual
Being gritty
Sending your kids to the best schools
Having a family
Having good friends
Helping others

Being popular in your community

Having low stress

Being athletic

Being adventuresome

Having a good sense of humor

Traveling the world

Being confident

Working hard

Being self-reliant

Being emotionally intelligent

Giving back to your community

Don't let yourself be limited by these short lists. Perhaps there are other values that you hold more closely in your life. Go deep and discover what is true for you.

Are you still with me? Good. I know people tend to skip exercises like this in books (I do, too), but this one is really worth the effort, so hang in there. Whittle down the list to the three or four values that are truly meaningful to you. Write them down. Your goal is to combine them into a single statement. Use these important values to draft a vision statement for yourself.

Once you have the short list of your most important personal core values, move on to step 2.

Step 2

Now ask yourself, *How does each core value play out in my life?* Think about your relationships, family, and loved ones. Think about work, achievement, and money. Think about health, fitness, and food. Think about self, spirituality, and purpose. Think about integrity, discipline, and honesty. Chances are that the virtues you might seek in one area transfer easily to other areas. When you consider all of these categories of your life, what are the core values that you'd like to see show up everywhere?

Step 3

Combine all of your thoughts and ideas into one definitive statement about what you value and how those values will play out in your day-to-day life. This is your true north. It doesn't have to be elegant or perfect; your statement just needs to accurately describe what motivates you and how that motivation manifests in your actions.

There, you did it. You now have a personal vision statement. Now that you have a clear sense of who you are and what your true north is, it is time to do this exercise with your whole family.

Live Your Values: For the Family

HOW TO DRAFT A VISION STATEMENT WITH YOUR FAMILY

Stephen R. Covey, author of the bestselling book *The 7 Habits of Highly Effective People*, describes a family vision statement as "a combined, unified expression from all family members of what your family is all about—what it is you really want to do and be—and the principles you choose to govern your family life."

A strong family vision statement is something everyone in the family can agree on. But equally important, it's something everyone can fall back on when faced with decisions that challenge their values. One of the most useful aspects of a vision statement is that it is an easy-to-remember guide for expected behavior within the family.

Ready to begin? Let's start with some basic guidelines. If you have very young kids, say, under six years of age, they may be a bit young for this exercise. Instead, just do this with your partner. When your kids are older and can contribute positively, you can try creating the vision statement as a whole family.

Do you already have teens or young adults and no family vision statement? It's never too late to do this. You may think they'll just roll their eyes if you suggest it, but don't be so sure. Each generation appreciates having a clear purpose. A recent study conducted by Imperative, Inc., in collaboration with the University of Michigan, Grinnell College, and Seattle Pacific University, surveyed 1,586 undergraduate students to gain insight into their predominant view of work and career. The survey found that 47 percent of students are purpose-driven, meaning they value the emotional satisfaction of working for a goal more than income or status. Surprised? This may surprise you even more: currently enrolled college kids are significantly more likely to be purpose-driven than college-educated workers. In addition, the study found that nearly a third of college students would rather declare "a purpose" than "a major."

As a parent, that should make you optimistic. It suggests that your kids may have a desire to lead a purpose-driven life. Drafting a family vision statement is one great way to find out. So let's get to it.

An effective vision statement should

- Be brief (no more than a short paragraph)
- Express the values your family holds dear
- Be proactive and motivational in tone
- Be easy to grasp by everyone in the family, regardless of age (with the exception of infants and toddlers, of course; you can fill them in later)
- Be easy to remember; if it's catchy, all the better

Here are the steps for building a family vision statement as a group.

Step 1: Gather the whole family and brainstorm.

Call a family meeting. Block out an hour with no distractions so you can brainstorm as a family without hurry. Turn off the TV and put the cell phones out of sight. Grab note paper and pencils or, better yet, poster board and markers. Sit around a kitchen or dining room table. Then ask everyone to think about their values, dreams, goals, passions. Just jot down statements and ideas. You can use the lists above as conversation starters or find other lists online. There are no wrong answers. You're filling a bucket with ideas from which you will later hone your statement. Make sure everyone gets his or her say. And remember, it's important that everyone contributes to the discussion. The more the kids feel they are part of the process, the more likely they will be to embrace the result.

Step 2: When you're stuck, prime the pump.

Everyone is looking at one another? No one's talking? Get things rolling by writing this on the poster board:

As a family, we . . .

Now start writing down the values you share. Here are some examples:

- love one another unconditionally
- respect one another and the feelings of others
- treat others as we want to be treated
- are kind and generous

- help one another
- want to eat healthy food
- want to be physically active
- value education and learning
- love ice cream (remember, there are no wrong answers, especially from six-year-olds)
- like to have adventures
- value together time
- seek to discover God's purpose for us

Write down every idea, even if some of you disagree. There will be time for discussion and refinement. At this point, just get your thoughts down on paper.

If you get stuck, try posing a question to the group that will spark additional discussion and trigger great ideas. Here are some fun questions to consider:

- What kind of family do we want to be?
- What things are very important to us?
- How do we want to treat one another?
- How do we want to resolve our arguments and disagreements?
- How do we want to treat people outside our family?
- How do we want to have fun?
- How can we help support one another's individual goals?
- What do we cherish most about our family?
- What rituals and traditions do we want to make and keep?
- How do we want to help other people?

As you can see, that's a lot to think about, and these questions will generate a lot of ideas. That's good. You may find that an hour has flown by. This exercise is important, and you may not get it done in one sitting. If so, schedule another family meeting to review and consolidate your ideas and start the process of whittling it all down.

Step 3: Write a draft vision statement.

Gather all of the ideas your family has come up with, and begin to organize them into a concise statement. You probably won't nail it on your first effort, so don't try to be perfect. Just get some lines down, then edit, revise, and hone. Make sure everyone takes part. How you write your statement isn't set in stone. You might create a motto, a jingle, a poem, or a credo. Be creative. But here's one rule you must follow: your statement needs to be easy to remember. If it's too long and complicated, you won't refer to it and it won't be useful. Once your family settles on the final draft, give yourselves a cheer and celebrate with some hugs and healthy treats. If you have a young artist in the family, you might even have him or her create an illustration or image to go with your motto.

Step 4: Use it, live it.

The most important step is putting your vision statement into action. Bring the family vision statement to the front and center in your daily life. Display it on the refrigerator, or post it on the bathroom mirror where your family will see it regularly.

Acknowledge when someone has put your family's values into play. If your child helps a friend in need, tell him or her that you are pleased. If your family takes a rigorous hike up a local mountain, fist-bump at the summit and snap a photo. The more you identify how your family is living its vision, the more integrity the whole family will feel.

There's one more action that's part of this critical fourth step: revisions—or, even better, re-envisions. From time to time, especially as your children get older, you may need to adjust your vision statement as a family. Your goals and values may change. Adapt. A vision statement should be strong but somewhat flexible to account for changing conditions.

LIVE YOUR VALUES (DON'T JUST PREACH THEM)

Be your child's best role model by living your family's values in all sectors of your life—in your career and as a parent, spouse, and friend.

Even when you don't think your kids are watching, they will notice and learn from your example, even at the earliest of ages. If you want your kids to see the value and joy in physical activity, then you must commit yourself to exercise and taking care of your body. If you want your kids to understand the value of taking care of things and picking up after themselves, pick up your own messes. Do the dishes. Don't leave a pile of clothing on the bathroom floor after a shower. Dad, if you want your daughters to feel empowered and value respect, treat your wife with respect, kindness, and love. (You'll be showing your sons how to respect women, too.) This approach becomes even more obvious when you consider the reverse equation: Should you expect your children to exhibit behavior that you are not exhibiting yourself? Can you appropriately lecture your child about the dangers of smoking if you smoke? Can you expect them to eat an apple when you are eating an ice cream sundae?

Modeling your values outside the home is essential for integration. It's one thing to have integrity in the walls of your home, but you need to take that integrity with you when you head out, too. If you want your kids to demonstrate respect for other people, like wait staff, laborers, police officers, and other service workers, you must first demonstrate that respect. If you want them to develop empathy, you must show compassion for those around you, contribute to the community, do volunteer work, and encourage your children to join you. This is your best opportunity to help your children develop character traits like integrity, honor, commitment, and compassion that will serve them in all aspects and phases of life. If you relish your leadership role, you will find that many of those leadership traits will rub off on your kids organically. You've heard it before: walk the walk; don't just talk the talk.

A NOTE ON COLLABORATION

There are all kinds of families out there: single-parent households, blended families, kids who are being raised without their parents in the picture. I know how lucky Courtney and I are to have what we have, and I understand that in this day and age we may seem like the quintessential family. A quick note on partnerships that aren't as symbiotic: it's common for parents to have different value systems. If you and your partner have opposing ideas of what's best for the family— you send the kids out to do the chores and your partner greets them with Cheetos and gummy bears when they're done—it's time for a hearty conversation. Here's where you get *curious*, which is one of Dr. L's favorite words. "It's not uncommon for family systems to disagree on things," she says, "but how they disagree and whether they can be curious together is the key to turning two opposing values into one working system. First, respect is key. Don't put down your partner's values. It will get you nowhere. Second, be curious together. Ask, *What is it about this value that matters to you?* For example, you might find that the super annoying behavior of gummy bear distribution after chores all comes from your partner's value of 'rewarding hard work.' Wow! Maybe you both can agree that this is important and then figure out how to weave in the value but modify the behavior so it's not in conflict with other values. Third, flex. You may feel that all of your values are the most important, but remember that you and your partner are a working dyad that needs some kind of balance. You have to be able to flex."

Out Doing Things
Sir Richard Branson

Sir Richard Branson, an English-born business magnate, author, and philanthropist, is the founder of the Virgin Group, which controls more than four hundred compa-

nies. He discovered he wanted to become an entrepre-
neur at a very young age.

If [my mother] felt that it was reasonably safe and we
were two miles from somewhere, she would push us
out of the car and tell us to make our own way. She
would have been arrested today if she would have
done that but she was a great believer in challenging us. She would not let us watch television. We had
to be out there doing things. So, life was that much
more fun. My mom would put us on a bike and tell us
to ride 100 miles somewhere. There's always a risk
when parents do that with their kids—my mother always had a backup plan—but the alternative, wrapping them up in cotton wool and not letting them get
out and play, is very sad.

In Conclusion

This true north exercise isn't a gimmick. As you develop your family
vision statement and start putting it into action, you will begin to see
its power. You'll be a family that sticks to a set of well-defined beliefs
and goals and behaviors that give structure and greater purpose to
all aspects of your family life. I know because it's working for my
family.

There will be times when someone in the family slips off track.
Sometimes this happens because your kid turns into a teenager and
no longer prioritizes the family virtue of "time together." That's natural. Kids—and adults for that matter—will go through ebbs and flows
with how committed they feel to the values. What's important is that

you keep in mind your children's development but maintain what's important. Don't let your kids run the show and bulldoze over the values that you've all decided on together just because they are going through a phase. Your true north and vision statement should not waver easily like leaves that fall off a tree when the weather gets cold. Your family's values are the roots that maintain the tree.

Fail Forward

Learn to Embrace Falling in the Mud

> To make no mistakes is not in the power of man; but from
> their errors and mistakes the wise and good learn wisdom
> for the future.
>
> —Plutarch

I t was a beautiful spring day when I set out with my four kids, my
buddy, and his two girls to hike into Squamish territory between
Vancouver and Whistler in British Columbia. This friend knew of a
cabin we could use near the peak of Squamish Mountain, so that became our goal. We hadn't done a whole lot of provisioning, but we did
stop at a sandwich shop at the base of the mountain to pick up some
food, and at Canadian Tire to pick up a few essentials so we could stay
overnight at the cabin. My friend is really laid back and he'd done the
hike before, so I thought this was going to be a tame day. We didn't
know what Mother Nature had in store.

When we were about five hours from the car, admiring the absolutely breathtaking view, I spotted a group of people, apparently a

well-coordinated team, ahead. They were wearing glacier goggles and were armed with ice picks, and they told us it would be another *seven hours* to the cabin. "You'll never make it there," one of them told us. I asked my buddy, "Where's this cabin?" and he said, "Not that far." It was a perfectly sunny, beautiful spring day, so I assumed it would be okay, and we kept going.

We hiked a little farther, and suddenly, we were knee-deep in snow. How was that possible? It was still hot out and really, really sunny.

"Where is your jacket?" I asked six-year-old Alex, my youngest daughter. She said she left it in the car. I noticed that my buddy's daughter was wearing little slip-on shoes. Soon, it started getting dark, the snow began to fall, and before we knew it, we were in a full-blown blizzard. We were about six hours from the car, and many hours from the cabin. The visibility was terrible. My daughters, Alex and Catherine, were huddled under one big sweater. One of my buddy's kids was having a meltdown because her feet felt like ice blocks. The kids were all slipping in the snow. And then Charlie, whose chops I've been busting since he was a toddler, showed me a whole other side of himself that's amazing. I was pulling a sled I got from Canadian Tire loaded with the little bit of gear we had, and he took the rope and pulled it with me. He ate ice for hydration and kept going. I thought to myself, *My God, if I were stranded in the Antarctic like Shackleton, this is the kind of person I'd want with me.* He had a quiet confidence about him that radiated the fact that he'd done all of this before: the walk, the snow, the dark, the cold. Charlie was the hero of the day.

That said, all of my kids walked many miles in a storm until we finally got to the cabin at 2 a.m. We slept like rocks and headed out of there the next day, blazing down the mountain to the car.

I am an imperfect person, leader, and parent. When I think about failure, it is stories like these that flash before my eyes. Why didn't I do more research into the mountain we were climbing, the path, and our destination? Why didn't I spend more time looking into the weather? Why didn't I grill my friend on some of the details of this hike and how long every leg would take? Why didn't I make sure my kid had her coat, or the other kid had the right shoes? That day could have taken a really bad turn—and this is one story of a hundred I could pull out of my brain at any moment. Failures, more than successes, tend to stick around. They loop in our mind over and over. But if we learn to shift perspective on our failures, this loop provides an opportunity for us to gain wisdom. This is how we fail forward.

I'll tell you who doesn't think of that day as a failure: Charlie. If Charlie thinks of it at all, he likely remembers it as a fantastic walk in the snow with his family, an exciting trip into the outdoors. Just another challenge, another test that gave him an opportunity to explore his skills as a leader. One person's failure can be another person's success. This is the beauty of failing—it's all about how we interpret it.

If you get nothing else from this book, know that our ability to face obstacles and fail forward and learn from mistakes is success in disguise. That's right, failing is succeeding. I know this because the more I witness people run away from what is uncomfortable, difficult, and challenging, the greater the instances of depression, bad health, and generational dysfunction. I'm no scientist, but I know enough from my work over the last few decades, running toward tough stuff and encouraging those around me to do the same, that life gets better when you fail. When we go to great lengths to ensure that we avoid any failure for ourselves—a project bomb at work, a DNF (Did Not Finish) at a race, a botched new routine—we make it impossible to live satisfying lives. What's worse? When we train our kids to avoid failure—receiving a bad grade, missing a layup at basketball, getting cut from a team, or breaking up with a friend—we cripple them. The opposite (for you and your kids, coworkers, colleagues, friends, and loved ones) is failing forward.

I definitely made some mistakes that day, but it's interesting to me when I consider how Charlie got to be such a resilient and capable little badass. He certainly failed a few times before he figured out how to be prepared and how to persevere. His resiliency rises to the surface because he has learned (and is still learning) how to fail and overcome, fail and overcome.

Failure leads to smarts like the kind Charlie demonstrated that day. Sure, Charlie doesn't think of that day as a failure, but I'm sure my other kids do to a certain extent. I know I do. But within that cold, imperfect, uncontrolled, humbling, grueling, and exciting day, my kids discovered at least some measure of their own resilience. They failed forward, and so did I.

We cannot keep ourselves in warm, perfectly controlled environments like hothouse flowers. We can't plan every moment or protect ourselves and the people around us from bruises and pain. We have to head out into the unpredictability of the real world, the natural world. We have to take risks and solve problems in real time. We need to learn to go with what life serves up, even if that's discomfort and difficulty and, yes, *failure*.

Sometimes you have to get a few bad grades before you learn how to get an A. You have to forget your coat to realize you never want to forget your coat again. Failing forward means committing to not making the same mistake again. It means using failure as fuel for building true resilience.

That day on Squamish Mountain was a rite of passage for my kids, a touchstone they still talk about today. You'd think they'd never want to do something like that again, but soon they were asking me, "Dad, when's the next hike?"

Decades of research into mindset and self-limiting behavior by psychologist Carol Dweck have shown that people's attitudes toward their failures come from the web of stories they tell themselves. Either we believe failure is to be avoided at all costs because it reflects that we're worthless or we believe that failure is an inevitable part of learning, something to be reflected on with curiosity and even appreciated. Furthermore, how we think about and talk about failure in our own lives impacts how our kids, and others who look up to us, think about it, too.

Some thirty years ago, Dweck coined the terms "fixed mindset" and "growth mindset." She explains her theory in the bestselling book *Mindset: The New Psychology of Success.* When you have a fixed mindset, Dweck says, you believe skills and abilities are something you either have or you don't, and you really can't change. Have you ever said to yourself, *I'll never be an athlete* or *I'm not a math person* or *I can't possibly do x, y, or z*? If you're wondering whether you have a fixed mindset, think about the narrative running through your mind. If that narrative is holding you back, it's because it stems from some pretty fixed ideas and self-imposed limitations. Beliefs about our potential develop from stories in our mind, Dweck argues. And they keep us in a fixed state, holding us back in life.

The polar opposite is the growth mindset. If you're operating from a growth mindset, you believe that skills are built and earned. You're not born with them, but you can develop them. You believe you are in control of your destiny. You can work for that promotion and succeed in getting it because your future isn't fixed. You can do a triathlon, even though you've never been a strong swimmer. You can not only persevere through a lockdown but get stronger in the process.

That's what you want for yourself and for your kids, right? You want them to think, *I can do it.* You want them to adopt that "I can't, until I can" attitude more often. It all starts and ends with the growth mindset.

Imagine that an entry-level coworker comes into your office and states a financial goal that he has for himself or for the team. Maybe he wants to increase profitability by 10 percent over last year, when the most you've ever done as a group is 5 percent. Maybe in your mind you're thinking, *That'll never happen. That's too ambitious.* But then you look at this young employee and ask yourself, *Why would I put a limit on someone who wants to achieve and improve? This is the kind of fire-in-the-belly attitude I* want *for my team.*

Same idea, different scenario. Imagine your daughter comes home and says she wants to learn Mandarin Chinese. Instead of blowing it off as too daunting or limiting her desire for a challenge, you simply encourage her. She practices and practices and eventually learns how to pronounce *nǐhǎo* (hello—pronounced *nee how*), *xièxiè* (thank you—*shieh-shieh*), and *bù kèqì* (you're welcome—*boo kuh-chi*). Her belief leads to action, which leads to growth. And growth strengthens the belief that she can do what seems impossible. Next thing you know, she'll be suggesting a tour of Beijing for your next family vacation. The growth mindset understands that intelligence is not a fixed trait and that skills can be grown over time.

Give yourself the perspective you would give that entry-level employee or your daughter. Here's a great exercise suggested by Dweck. Whenever you work through something difficult, imagine your brain is actually growing. Try to picture the connections firing off like electromagnetic waves as you rise to meet challenges and learn.

Growth Mindset Versus Fixed Mindset

Growth Mindset

"I like to learn new things."

"Failure will help me grow."

"I welcome feedback because I can learn from it."

"Adversity helps me become smarter."

"I like to try things that make me nervous."

"My attitude and hard work determine what I can do."

Fixed Mindset

"I'm either good at it or not good at it."

"Failure shows me the limits of my abilities."

"I can't do certain things."

"I wasn't built to do that."

"I don't like doing things I'm not good at."

"When I'm frustrated, I give up because there's no point."

"Why put in the effort when nothing will ever change?"

"I take criticism personally."

Dweck wants us to know that we are not just either fixed thinkers or growth thinkers. We're a mix. Our attitude can change by the day, by the hour, by the challenge ahead of us, and by our mood. That understanding is something you'll want to teach your kids, too. It's human nature to doubt yourself, especially when trying new things or when situations aren't going your way. The key is developing a belief that no matter what is thrown at us we do have some control over outcomes, and we can, with time and effort, get better and do better.

Dweck writes: "If parents want to give their children a gift, the best thing they can do is to teach their children to love challenges, be intrigued by mistakes, enjoy effort, and keep on learning. That way, their children don't have to be the slaves of praise. They will have a lifelong way to build and repair their own confidence."

And that's where the gift of adversity comes in. Overcoming adversity builds confidence and resilience. Adversity teaches you what you are capable of and feeds a growth mindset, just as it did for Catherine, Alex, Charlie, and the rest of the crew on that snowy Squamish mountain.

Fail Forward:
For the Family

HOW TO BUILD A GROWTH MINDSET:
TRUST PLUS ACTION EQUALS GROWTH

Tiffany Smiley is an entrepreneur, advocate, speaker, wife of a wounded veteran, and mother of three boys. Her husband, Scotty Smiley, was leading a platoon in Mosul, Iraq, in 2005 when a suicide bomber detonated a device; shrapnel left him blind and temporarily paralyzed. Major Smiley woke up at the Walter Reed Army Medical Center outside Washington, DC, a week later. With faith and determination and a lot of support from Tiffany, Scotty rebuilt his life, becoming the first blind active-duty officer in military history.

Tiffany worked very hard to make sure her sons never saw a disability in Scotty. They only saw what he was capable of, and they grew to believe that anything is possible. "Parents need to show their kids how much they can accomplish. To do that you have to put them in situations where they don't feel capable," she says. For example, she made her kids join the elite swim team in town. "It's really competitive. You have to know every stroke. I thought, 'Perfect, I'm here to watch my children fail.' I wanted our boys to experience feeling insecure and vulnerable and not good at something." Sure enough, her son Grady didn't know how to do the butterfly well. After practice, the coach walked over and said to Tiffany, "I'm sorry to say this, but Grady's butterfly stroke is terrible." Later that day, Grady turned to his mom and said, "I heard what the coach said." Tiffany waited to see if her son would get upset. Instead, he looked up at her and said, "Well, I'm going to have to learn that stroke."

This is a growth mindset in action. We can pivot from failure and criticism to trusting ourselves and engaging in action, and eventually to growth. We can set our sights on something difficult and chase down that goal.

How do you plant the seeds for a growth mindset in your children? Here are six universal ways to do it. The overarching lesson is this: trust (believing you can grow) + action (practice, repetition, and the adversity that comes with any action over time) = growth (true resilience).

1 ***Build future belief by reflecting on past wins.*** When your kid says, "I can't learn to do the backstroke," remind her of past learning experiences and accomplishments, those resilience data points! Say, "Wait a minute, didn't you learn the breaststroke last season? What else have you learned how to do that was just as hard? How about learning that tough Beethoven piece on the piano? Didn't you work hard at that? Remember how good you felt after performing it at the recital?" Remind your kid that no one is great at anything when they are first learning the skill. Even prodigies had to figure out they had a skill. Call up past examples of success that remind your kids of their capacity for learning.

Encourage them to give themselves credit for past accomplishments. It will help them build up the critical part of the growth mindset called "belief."

2 **Teach them to be curious.** When your kids are really curious about something, inhibitions and limitations fall away. Curiosity, at its core, is the nitro fuel for action. Foster curiosity in your children by exploring new experiences and being aware of the sparks of interest that can grow into passion. Encourage your kids to wonder, to never be hesitant to ask questions, to explore, and to fully experience the world. Don't shoo them away with a dismissive response even if they ask you a random question that you can't possibly answer, like "What would it be like to have six arms?" Encourage their outlandish curiosity through total participation in their discovery. Say, "I don't know. What do you think it would be like?" That may sound like a silly example, but the more curiosity you foster early on, the better. You want your kids to become students of life. The most successful people never stop learning and growing.

3 **Set high goals.** Stretch goals will virtually guarantee some level of failure and the heartache that comes with it. That's where the real learning starts. Don't be timid about pushing your kids. Believe me, they are way tougher than you can imagine. Set the bar high. If they miss the bar, good. Great, in fact. Make sure they recognize that failure as an opportunity to learn and gain wisdom. Dr. L says, "Every time they fail, ask them, 'How did you fail forward here?'

Teach them what this means and have them speak the language more and more." If they hit their goal, great. Celebrate the win and then ask them what their next goal is. If they want the same goal, push them to set the bar higher. Don't let your own limiting beliefs or fear of whether they can hit it stand in the way.

4   ***Show them the power of constructive criticism.***
No one likes being criticized or corrected. Kids often take it personally, like it's a black eye on their character. It's really important to show your kids that when a coach or teacher corrects them, it should be thought of as a gift. It's a special hint that they can use to get better. And that's what the coach or teacher wants—a better outcome for their benefit. Tell your children that coaches and teachers wouldn't correct them if they didn't care about making them a better player or student. Practice healthy criticism in your home so that your children can get used to hearing things that may make them uncomfortable. For example, if your son sets the table and everything is wonky, nothing in the right place, and he turns to you and says, "I'm not good at this." Respond with, "You may not be great at it yet, so let's look at where you went wrong and see if we can fix it." You don't always have to sugarcoat it by saying, "This is amazing! What are you talking about?!" Be thoughtfully honest and constructive with your children. It will serve them better down the road; as adults, when they encounter constructive criticism at their job, in their marriage, or with

friends, they'll be able to tolerate it, take it in, and make corrections.

5 *Try something new every week.* How will your daughter know she doesn't like soccer or rock climbing or brussels sprouts for that matter if she doesn't give them a shot? Trying new things is the surest way to build a growth mindset in your kids. The more they try new things, the more opportunity they have to stumble and fail, laugh it off, get back up, and cultivate their skills. If you have older kids, you might talk to them about "brain plasticity," which is the science of how your brain can grow and expand at any age. Like any muscle in your body, your brain grows new cells and connections when it is challenged with learning new things. Have your kids brush their teeth with their nondominant hand tonight. It feels weird. It's hard. But if they do it for a week straight, it wouldn't seem so foreign. That's brain plasticity at work, and it's an incredible muscle that we need to flex more. When we create new neural pathways, we are literally building a more resilient brain! The same sort of thing happens when you learn a new language or a new skill, like playing guitar. You can remodel your brain, too, even at the advanced age of twenty-five, fifty-five, or eighty-five. Tell your kids you'll learn how to do a TikTok dance if they'll learn how to waltz or polka.

6 *Use what they are learning in school to emphasize the value of adversity.* Throughout elementary and middle school, your kids are going to be studying the history of the United States. They are going to

learn about the founding of our nation, slavery, the tragedy of the Civil War, World War II, and the horrors of the Holocaust. Be aware of what your children are reading and studying. Ask questions about what they're discussing in class, and use those talks as opportunities to point out how individuals and nations grew through struggle and how people have consistently triumphed over adversity. There is much to learn about the human spirit from our collective history.

For most of our time on earth, we had to protect our young to ensure the survival of the human race. Today, that is less of an issue, but we are still being guided by legacy software in our parenting code. We mean well. We love our kids, and we will do almost anything to help them succeed. Your complete investment in your child is admirable and not to be minimized.

But be careful. Investment and dedication can quickly turn into our own attachment to a fixed mindset. Growth is about failure and not always knowing the ending. That can be scary as a parent, so sometimes we operate from a more fixed position, resisting our child's request to try something new. Take notice of that. "Out of love and desire to protect our children's self-esteem, we have bulldozed every uncomfortable bump and obstacle out of their way, clearing the manicured path we hoped would lead to success and happiness," writes educator Jessica Lahey in her insightful bestselling book, *The Gift of Failure*. "The setbacks, mistakes, miscalculations, and failures we have shoved out of our children's way are the very experiences that teach them how to be resourceful, persistent, innovative and resilient citizens of this world." Bingo.

We fail as parents when we fail to allow our children to develop a growth mindset and experience the struggle that comes along with it. Dr. L confirms this and says she sees it play out every day in her private practice when working with parents and their children. She relates that most of her clients aren't "bad" parents. In fact, some are the most loving, invested, and engaged parents on the planet. But their demonstration of love somehow gets mutated into a giant hustle for perfection, which leads to overparenting. She suggests valuing process over product—it's how you got somewhere that matters, not *that* you got there in the first place.

When Overparenting Backfires: A Cautionary Tale

Dr. Lara Pence

I've worked with many adolescents over the course of my career, but one continues to haunt me as a glaring example of how a parent's pursuit of protection can turn into a disaster. Kelly (name has been changed for privacy purposes) was a senior in high school and applying to college. There was one school in particular that she had her heart set on. Since middle school, Kelly had attached herself to the colors of the University of Texas and waited for the day when she could walk the campus as a UT student. She had all the UT gear, including the UT bumper sticker, and she made the "hook 'em horns" gesture as her greeting when she entered my office. Initially, Kelly was referred to me because of her anxiety, but she also struggled with some self-esteem issues and perfectionistic tendencies, a common presenting struggle among young people of her age.

When it came time for Kelly to apply to UT, her GPA fell just below the automatic acceptance threshold for a Texas resident, and so she labored over the application process. She arrived in my office one day looking particularly forlorn and mentioned that her parents had decided they would take over the application and complete it for her. I probed for further information, and Kelly revealed that not only had her mother decided to write her essays for her, but that she had also concocted a story that Kelly had once had a sibling with cancer who had recently passed away. None of this was true. When I asked her how she felt about her parents' actions, she shrugged sadly and said, "They don't think I'm interesting enough, I guess."

Knowing the parents, I had no doubt that their decision to complete her application was one of protection. They simply felt that they could do a better job, her application would most likely be accepted, and they would shield her from the heartache of rejection and failure. But that's not how Kelly saw it. She received the message that she was boring, was not worthy of being accepted as she was, and was incapable of doing the work herself. Furthermore, she learned that failure was unacceptable and must be avoided at all costs, even if that meant lying on important documents. The whole thing was heartbreaking, but her own interpretation of what this meant about her was the most difficult to see. She felt like she wasn't good enough for her parents and that her parents didn't think she was good enough for UT.

When parents step in as a shield and hustle to prevent their kids from experiencing failure, they activate belief systems in their children that are hard to repair. *I'm not good enough on my own* and *Failure is unacceptable* are two of the most common. Consider whether you want your kid to have to unravel that big mess throughout their young adult and adult life, or just cry for an hour because the failure sucked. It's awful when your kid gets slapped in the face with a powerful and painful fail, but the alternative actually is worse. In all my years of working with kids, teens, and young adults, I've never heard one say, "I'm so grateful for my parents for protecting me from failure all those years." But I have absolutely heard the opposite: "If only they let me fail once in a while, I probably wouldn't be so fucked up!" or "They protected me from everything, and now I don't want to and can't do anything."

You may think this story has some kind of happy ending, but alas, it doesn't. Kelly was rejected from UT and did not attend her dream school.

In Conclusion

I don't expect nor do I want you to manufacture failure for yourself or your kids. There's enough failure in this world to go around. I also don't expect you to plunge into an icy river every morning, or to throw your kids in, or to take them on a hike in the middle of the night in a blizzard. However, I do hope that when they get tired, cold, or uncomfortable, you fight your first instinct to pick them up. You let them experience the struggle, let them work on that growth mindset, and begin to embrace the idea of failure. I realize that you want to give your kids the best leg up possible so that they have the greatest chance at success. What I'm asking you to do, however, is shift your perspective on what that leg up looks like. A leg up is not paving the way. A leg up is not seeing success at every turn or after every effort. A leg up is not teaching them that failure is bad and unacceptable. A leg up is shifting perspective on failure, leading them into difficult experiences so they can test their own mindset, and encouraging them to fail forward.

How can you implement this today? Start with a hike in the rain, and let your kids adapt to the beautiful unpredictability of nature. Have them make dinner, and no matter how awful it tastes, have a good laugh with them about the process. Tape up their latest bad grade on the fridge and have them write their failure mantra on it. Whether they're learning Mandarin, geometry, piano, public speaking, or the butterfly (by far the hardest stroke), push them to grow. Show them you trust the process, let them see your encouragement, and if they fail, let them see your interest in what they learned. And if they fail, at least they tried.

Dedicate to a Daily Routine

How Schedules Lead to Success

> If you want to change the world, start off by making your bed.
>
> —Admiral William H. McRaven

A s you know by this point, I'm a believer that the number one motivator for human beings is the avoidance of discomfort. Part of this is biological. Human existence depended on our recognition of pain, which enabled us to survive when we were exposed to the harsh realities of nature. If we didn't avoid discomfort, we would die. We would freeze in the snow or continue to eat toxic food. However, even today, when there is no immediate threat to our survival, we are always consciously, and even subconsciously, avoiding discomfort.

So here's the catch: to be healthy in the world today, you have to do what others aren't doing. We have become a society that promotes habits that are actually bad for us—regular drinking, overspending, eating cereal that looks like a rainbow. To be healthy in both mind and body, we often have to go against the grain and resist the distraction of shiny things, social media, and Saturday night cocktails. You have to do things that challenge your first instinct to fall in line with the norm and keep you comfortable. You have to zig when others zag, stick your neck out, lift heavy things, do endurance exercises, eat green foods, go to bed early, avoid alcohol. Otherwise, you risk sliding into the sick, sedentary, and solitary life that so many struggle with.

Unless someone is holding you accountable, or unless you're someone like myself (a bit of a maniac) and you've trained your mind to prefer discomfort, it is really hard for us to choose this path. I know because I see people who have every reason to want to change their lives for the better, but the instinct to avoid discomfort is like an invisible set of handcuffs keeping them tethered to sleeping through the alarm and eating junk food and skipping their workout. Dr. L sees this all the time, too, with clients who show up to her office miserable and suffering but unwilling to do the hard stuff that might make their lives more enjoyable.

Truth be told, your mind and body are probably craving some kind of change right now—why else would you have picked up this book in the first place? Maybe you sit all day long and want that tool that's going to get you moving. Or perhaps you've become obsessed with work and need to dial back in to your family but don't know how. You know that something is off, but you don't know what, and you're not sure where to start to activate real, sustainable change.

Real change starts with structure. The best thing you can do if you want to be someone who is more tolerant of discomfort, more willing to lean in to what's tough when others lean out, and more healthy overall, is to find a daily routine, set up a schedule, and stick to it. Write it down. Force yourself to do it.

Most people who end up at my farm training with me never intended to be overweight or undisciplined. However, at some point, they started to go through their lives moving from one task to the next without clear intention or dedication. They became controlled by cravings for comfort and uninspired to do much that challenges this comfort. The result of this aimless way of living is a schedule that suits your every feeling. You wake up when you want because you feel tired. You eat what you want because Oreo cookies provide relief. You drink when you want to take the edge off. You avoid workouts because you don't want to be sore. It's an endless pursuit of pleasure.

Does this sound familiar? You manage to show up to the gym for your workout, but you feel a little bit sluggish or didn't sleep well last night, so you jump on the treadmill for a few minutes until it hurts. Then you stop. Or you do some crunches until it starts to get uncomfortable. Then you stop. You check your phone and realize it's been eighteen minutes, and that's long enough for a workout, right?

Creating a daily schedule and a consistent routine is a surefire way to go from unmotivated to motivated and aimless to amazing. It holds you accountable to yourself. It keeps your day from being upended by passing feelings, cravings, and wants.

Routines Are More Than Just Physical

My routine is critical for my mental health. Going to sleep at the same time—early—means I know when I need to start shutting down the heavy sensory devices like screens and televisions. It also means I'm honoring my commitment to wake up at a certain time in the morning. You may hate getting up, but you never regret getting up. When you set a routine, it allows you to move through your day like a meditation. Inhale, exhale. This task, next task. All executed with steadiness and grace. You know when your day will end because you know when the next day has to begin. There's predictability and consistency to keep you in line with your next move.

I find that setting a routine also protects from the dreaded anxiety and burnout so many people face today. When parents were coming to me in the early months of the pandemic, worried about their kids and wearing that worry all over their faces and in their body language, I thought, *No wonder kids are complaining of anxiety so early in life. If we can't calm down, how will they?* It concerned me that many parents didn't consider a schedule as a solution to all the craziness. When everything felt so out of control in the beginning of the pandemic, a routine seemed like a simple way to at least find some predictability—and yet so many families opted out. Or they tried it for a few days, found that it was hard, and bailed.

The best antidote I've found for endless worry and anxiety is a commitment to the mundane tasks of a daily routine. Think about how you handle the anxiety of a busy day at work. You have a million emails coming your way, some deep work to get to, and more fires to put out with every phone call. So you create a checklist to guide you through your day.

I tackle anxiety-causing circumstances in much the same way as a busy workday. I commit to my day like a simple checklist:

Wake up at 5 a.m., check.
Functional fitness routine, check.
One hundred burpees for extra measure, check.
Five-minute breathing, check.

Returning to a checklist reminds us that whatever the larger world might be going through, we are personally responsible only for ourselves. I control what I do. Suddenly the anxiety-producing events on social media and in the news aren't relevant when all I'm committed to worrying about is the next thing on my checklist. I urge you to think of your life this way and see the results manifest.

If you work the night shift or are on call, or if you have a young family and are up multiple times a night, routine is tough. I get it. I remember those early mornings when our children were first born. Courtney typically woke up to feed the baby at 3 a.m., but I always found myself jolted awake by her movement and the baby's cries. I would try to settle back to bed, only to slide out eventually and see her walking around the baby's bedroom like a zombie, the two of us completely sleep-deprived. And then at 5 a.m., the alarm would go off and my day would officially start. Sometimes the best thing to do in tough times like these is to let the lack of routine *be* the routine. If sleeping in is a necessity a few times a week, make sure your daily routine still applies whether you get up at the scheduled time or you wake up later. This will keep you from being too hard on yourself if you miss your wake-up time because you're doing more important things—like helping your spouse keep the baby alive. If you're up at 5, great. You have more time to execute the tasks of the day. If you're up at 9, get started on those tasks just the same, realizing that you might not complete them until early evening. You can be flexible with timing when circumstances require, but maintaining consistency in the tasks themselves is important.

My Daily Routine

5:00 a.m.—wake up

5:15 a.m.—morning workout (I do the same functional fitness exercises everyday like clockwork)

5:45 a.m.—our dogs start barking and the parrot starts whistling; it's up and at 'em for the family!

6:00 a.m.—wake up the kids with Courtney, blast the classic rock, and get the family out the door

6:15 a.m.—work out with the kids, jog around the block, do sit-ups, push-ups, stretching, the usual

7:00 a.m.—shower and breakfast

7:30 a.m.—first meeting of the day with the team

8 a.m. to 4:30 p.m.—working, making shit happen (with a call or two to Courtney in between)

5:00 p.m.—home with the kids and quickly off to sports practice (wrestling, soccer, etc.)

6:00 p.m.—home for dinner

6:30 p.m.—evening workout and stretch

7:00 p.m.—help kids with Mandarin and math

8:30 p.m.—get kids to bed

9:00 p.m.—get off to bed myself

Don't Play Russian Roulette with Your Routine

Routine is difficult to establish in the best of times. So what happens when shit hits the fan?

One of the biggest challenges that people faced during the pandemic was maintaining some sense of routine. Our world was flipped upside down, and many people were forced to work from home. This brought about a whole slew of challenges because the additional freedom served as an excuse for many: alarm clocks could be snoozed, workouts could be postponed, takeout could be ordered, and pants became optional.

As a result, routines disappeared quickly. When the built-in structure that going to work provided was eliminated, we fell apart. But routines are *key*. Your brain craves and thrives on consistency. For kids, consistency is like a multivitamin that needs to be taken daily! If you make sure that your routines are ironclad and unwavering, you'll be less vulnerable to chaos and disruption.

Tips for Keeping Your Routine Ironclad

Make sure each task is measurable and achievable. Assign a length of time to your tasks, and make sure what you've established is doable. For example, ten minutes of meditation does not mean you have to execute the meditation with perfection, but you do need to sit still for those ten minutes and try. Those ten minutes are the task, not the perfection. The timeline makes it measurable. If, over time, you find you want to meditate longer, start increasing your time each day by one minute. That makes the task at hand achievable.

Start small. Remember how you eat an elephant? One bite at a time. Each of your tasks is a bite of that elephant. You don't want to drain yourself with each task, or you'll never make it through the day. If you keep the tasks small, they will amount to big achievements later on.

Don't wait. We all have excuses for not getting to this or that during our day. Believe me, I've heard every excuse there is. The washing machine broke. My shoulder hurts. I ate too much. I ate too little. It's raining. It's too sunny. When you make excuses, the only person you're letting down is you. Remember rule 3, Commit to No Bullshit.

Align your routine with your values. Lots of people have started routines and then stopped. Why? Because they don't attach it to a value. They don't know *why* they set the routine in the first place, other than "Well, Joe De Sena said so." That's not good enough if you want it to stick. Go back to your values, those principles that you picked earlier in the book. See if you can associate your morning routine with a value. Hard work is one of mine, and getting up before dawn each and every day is hard work. Maybe your value is honor. Does spending ten minutes scrolling through your Instagram feed first thing in the morning align with that value? Probably not. Instead, pick something that does, like creating a gratitude list.

Use structure. Dr. L recommends a template that can help with establishing and maintaining your routine. She uses one she calls the three Bs. Every morning ask: What is one thing I can do for my *brain*? One thing I can do for my *body*? And what is the next *best* step I can take toward a goal I am working on? Brain—meditation, body—burpees, next best step—get that first email off to my team. Bingo! If you don't use the three Bs, find another way to organize your routine so that it doesn't feel haphazard and chaotic. If it makes sense, you will be more consistent with it.

Take the tech out. Nothing in your morning routine should involve technology. Stay away from phones, TV, and iPads. Technology is an immediate distraction that leads to further distractions. If you include checking your email in your morning routine, what happens if you're notified of a sale for those new sneakers you've been eyeing? You'll be tempted to go down the shopping rabbit hole and abandon your routine. Don't do it. Take the tech out!

Don't forget your nighttime routine! What happens at night is at least as important as what happens in the morning. There is much data on the importance of good sleep, and consistency is key. If you head to bed at the same time every night, you are leaps and bounds ahead of the rest of society. You know the drill: keep the lights low, and don't look at screens in bed. But here's the kicker—there is no better way to get better sleep than to get yourself to bed on time. It might sound obvious, but I can't tell you how many people I meet who want a hack. There just isn't one. You just have to GO. TO. BED. You can't miraculously get the benefits of eight hours of good sleep by going to bed at midnight and waking up for work at 6. The math just doesn't add up. If you want better sleep, put in the work by sacrificing that extra Netflix show or that one last YouTube video, and hit the sack.

Dedicate to a Daily Routine: For the Family

At 6 every morning, it's my job to wake the kids up and get them going. I peel the covers back and yell, "Up and out!" and they moan or grumble. More than once, my daughters have hid in the closet and slept there to keep me from waking them up so early. It's a battle every single day. But I'm relentless. I take no prisoners. We start each morning focusing on our body—I find it clears their morning attitude and feeds them a whole bunch of endorphins to get the day started.

It's important that I have these predawn hours with my kids. In the heart of the day, I am running a business and they're at school. When I'm home and not traveling, we do a set of bodyweight drills in the mornings that they've been doing for years. Courtney and I supervise them, and I also work out myself. I've hired (and housed) coaches to keep them fit and to challenge the old fitness patterns they may already know. The bodyweight routines I prefer are full of functional fitness exercises like bear crawls, crab-walking, push-ups, squats, lunges, and burpees. If it snows, we might push sleds or drag chains in the snow. If we're in Vermont, we might hike up and down a muddy mountain trail carrying kettlebells or buckets or bricks. As my daughter Catherine says, "I hate getting up early, but I like being fast and strong."

When we eat breakfast, they're not eating Cocoa Puffs while I eat a veggie omelet or oatmeal. They eat what Courtney and I eat, which always involves a lot of fruit, vegetables, and other real foods. They see me doing morning chores, like making my bed, and they do their own while our parrot watches (and squawks) over us. What I demand of them, I demand of myself. I see these mornings as a way for me to integrate my kids into my daily life. I want to be a model for them every day, and to do that I have to be in their line of sight.

I've always involved my kids in Spartan races and competitions of all kinds, so they see me in the context of my work and my life's mission. As soon as they could, my kids ran with me. Jack did the Boston Marathon with me at age eight, and Charlie did the New York Marathon at age seven. We ran them alongside the actual participants, as it would have been hard for either to actually qualify, but they got it done. Catherine did a Spartan Beast (a half marathon with thirty obstacles) beside me at age six! She wasn't wearing the right shoes and she was in agony, but she pushed through.

I recognize that the life I've created affords me a lot of freedom to be with my kids. However, I've worked on Wall Street and in the service industries of pool cleaning and construction, so I know what it is to have a job that exhausts you with demands or keeps you in a chair all day. I understand that often you want to come home and collapse on the couch and drown your stress in a bag of chips, a beer, or a streaming service. You might want to zone out, but don't, if only because *your kids are watching you*. The life you lead will become their blueprint for how a healthy adult is supposed to live. Rip yourself off the couch, and they will follow. Teaching your kids to have a routine is all about being a role model. Their little brains are craving consistency and a sense of predictability in life (especially now that you're going to let them engage in more challenging experiences!), and a routine is a good way to help kids build structure. But you can't just tell them—you have to show them. Kids retain only a fraction of what you say to them, but they pay attention to everything you do. *Everything*. During the first two years of life, imitation is the vital tool for developing language and social skills. That's Child Psych 101. But as your kids grow, they don't stop mimicking your actions. Kids—from toddlers to teens—are constantly watching you, even when you don't realize it. They're looking, listening, and absorbing your every move, like little hungry sponges. Psychologists, Dr. L included, say it's actually a crucial part of their journey toward independence. It's how they understand that you are you and they are them. Let's take a look at five key ways you can model good—or bad—behavior for your kids.

1. MODELING GOOD LIFESTYLE CHOICES

Lifestyle habits are an easy way to model behavior. If you want your kids to start smoking cigarettes and drinking, go ahead, have a cigarette and a few beers on the patio. If you want your kids to become obese, hit the drive-through for dinner every night, then pass out on the couch. Don't want that for your kids? Then put down those chips and eat some carrots. You are not going to get them to voluntarily choose broccoli if you are always snacking on cake.

If you want your kids to exercise, *you* need to exercise. If you want your kids to make their beds, make *your* bed. If you want them to be nice to others, model acts of kindness and respect for others every day. Say thank you to the grocery clerk. Help someone change a flat tire in the rain. Tip your waiter and waitress well when they've done a good job, and explain to your kids why that matters.

Behavioral psychologists have always known that children learn by imitating adults. Young chimpanzees do it, too. But unlike the imitation of apes, human copycat behavior has another purpose beyond learning a practical task. It helps develop and transmit human culture.

Several years ago, anthropologists from Australia and South Africa studied Australian preschoolers and the children of Kalahari San in southern Africa. The two groups were chosen because of distinct differences in parenting styles. In the experiments, the adults showed the kids the way to open a box using a complicated method; they used a stick to pull on a knob even though it would have been faster and easier to simply use their fingers to pull the knob. Despite the fact that the children were allowed to play with the box and discover the easy method, the majority of the children, both Australian kids and Kalahari kids, mimicked exactly what the adults did, using the more complicated method to open the box. The researchers believe this may be part of how humans develop and share culture. Children are motivated to do things like their parents because they want to be like us.

This example proves one thing to me as a father: I had better model the kind of behavior I want my kids to adopt. But let's be clear—we aren't just talking about removing salty snacks from the pantry and becoming more physically active. We are also talking about modeling emotional responsibility.

2. MODELING EMOTIONAL RESPONSIBILITY AND LITERACY

When we are emotionally responsible, we are aware of our feelings in times of high stress, and we regulate our responses. When we're not aware of what is happening internally, we end up operating from a reactionary position and often make poor choices. This happens for many people when someone cuts them off on the highway and the adrenaline surge pushes them to chase after the offenders. Or when your kid tests your patience all the way to the brink and you lash out in anger, yelling or slamming doors. The message you're sending is that it's okay to act out when you are pissed off. You're confirming to your kid that losing your temper is an acceptable or even appropriate response. Why, then, are you surprised if your teen says, "Fuck you," and slams the door when you tell him to be home before curfew?

If you want emotionally responsible kids who don't fly off the handle whenever they are frustrated, hurt, or angry, then you have to show them how to respond to adverse conditions. This is a tough skill for kids to learn. Like a new language, it takes practice and patience. They have to learn to recognize the rising rage inside and to slow down the adrenaline rush in order to have the time to reason with a clear head and decide on an emotionally responsible way to act.

This is one of the most important skills you can model for your kids. Why? Research shows that children who are less impulsive are also less likely to have mental health issues, abuse drugs and alcohol, and be vulnerable to abusive relationships. Hand in hand with emotional responsibility is emotional literacy—you have to get your kids more comfortable with a wide range of emotions. Dr. L says that one good way to do this is to expand your own emotional vocabulary and encourage your kids to do the same. "*Fine* and *okay* mean nothing to me," she says. "So when I pick my kids up from school and ask, 'How was your day?' I won't settle for those two words. Or even *good*. They've got to tell me more. Use more emotional language with your kids—ask if they felt proud, scared, disappointed, excited, uncertain, embarrassed—and ask yourself the same."

Here's an example of what real-world modeling can do for a family. One summer, my friend Tom and his family were traveling through Ireland. Not used to driving on the opposite side of the road, Tom pulled a little too close to the sidewalk in a small seaside town, scraped the curb, and busted both left tires. His family was not happy with him. His teenagers were hangry, and they knew this snafu was going to delay the next meal. But it was worse than that. The car only had one spare tire, and of course two were needed. It was late Sunday afternoon, and there wasn't a service station open within sixty miles. "OMG, we're going to have to sleep in the car," the kids whined. "Maybe," Tom said, smiling, "but let's find a place to eat first."

The family easily located a small restaurant that not only made the best cod and chips they had ever eaten but also featured traditional Irish music. The live band was amazing. The people were friendly. And the bartender hooked the family up with a local woman who let them stay at an empty cottage for the night for next to nothing. In the morning, they discovered that the cottage was right on the water in a beautiful setting. While Tom arranged for two new tires, his wife canceled their hotel reservation as the family had decided to stay put for another two nights. The burden of car trouble turned into a wonderful opportunity for the whole family because Tom embraced the dilemma with a positive attitude and decisive action.

But is there an age when kids are just too young to get this idea of regulating their emotions and managing their responses? Teenagers, after all, are different from toddlers. I asked Dr. L about the best age to start teaching emotional responsibility. "Age does play a significant role," she said. "The younger they are, the more primal their initial response may be, but even kids as young as three can begin learning emotional regulation skills like taking a deep breath or pausing or calming their body. We want to help a kid's brain develop and gain muscle memory for emotion regulation, not wait until their brain is 'developed' and then teach it. So, start young."

Dr. L added, "Make sure you are paying particular attention to your responses around the emotion of disappointment because, in life, being disappointed can't be avoided. When you experience disappointment, ensure that you are modeling resilience and flexibility. Say something like 'I'm disappointed, but I'll make the best of it.'"

If you notice that your children's disappointed feelings are turning them into monsters, help them understand that we all feel disappointment, but this doesn't mean we're allowed to be disrespectful, unkind to others, or destructive. Talk about the importance of pausing and taking a break to recalibrate. Sit with your children and actually do some deep breathing together. Your kids can learn, if you show them what to do.

3. MODELING FINANCIAL RESPONSIBILITY

Charlie recently asked me for money to start a lawn-mowing business. I liked his thinking. I made him agree to mow the fields of a local school before I would finance his mower. I think he pictured something like a sweet tractor, but when we went to the store, I pointed to the most basic hand mower so that he would understand that he'd have to save up and sweat to get a nicer mower. Nothing should be given that's not earned.

You see, part of our job as parents is to teach our kids about money—working hard to earn it, save it, manage it, share it, and spend it responsibly. Your own relationship with money will substantially influence your kids' relationship with money as they grow older. Remember rule 2, Earned, Not Given? It applies here as well. Remind your kids that you *earn* the money that you make and therefore you take care of it, spend it wisely, and don't ever take it for granted.

"More is caught than taught," says personal finance and business guru Dave Ramsey, a bestselling author and nationally syndicated radio host. He adds, "What your kids see you do is a lot more powerful than what they hear you say." Ramsey and his daughter Rachel Cruze, who hosts her own radio show, wrote a book that's worth checking out. It's called *Smart Money Smart Kids: Raising the Next Generation to Win with Money.* In the book, Rachel talks about how her parents' words and actions came together as a consistent message to demonstrate their family's value system. "Church was important to my family, and my parents have tithed to the church my entire life," she writes. "Every Sunday, I watched Mom and Dad put a folded check in the red velvet offering bag as people passed it down the pew. That image is burned in my mind even now as an adult. No matter how much we were struggling financially, no matter how big or small Dad's paycheck was, Dad and Mom put a check in that bag every single week. Because we watched Mom and Dad give, we knew that one of our family values was to give a percentage of whatever money we made. So even as kids, that's what we did."

4. MODELING IMPERFECTION

Another important way to model healthy attitudes and actions you would like your children to embody is to demonstrate that you are not perfect. We all know that no one does the right thing all the time, but a lot of parents fall into the trap of trying to be the hero mom or super dad who never makes a mistake. They think their kids will respect (and listen to) them more if they seem to be infallible. Bad move. Your kids will want to achieve perfection to gain your love. It simply amplifies their fear of screwing up. They'll shut down. They'll avoid failure and anything that might end with a less-than-perfect outcome. They'll hide stuff—poor grades, fights with friends, water they accidentally spilled in their room. Since it's impossible to be "perfect," modeling this false goal will make your kids' lives miserable. It's much wiser to show your kids that you are human, you make mistakes, and you know how to own and learn from those mistakes.

There are lots of different ways that you can model imperfection. Dr. L has a great suggestion: If you find yourself responding to your children in a way that isn't productive—

voice too loud, tone too stern, response incongruent with what's just occurred—circle back and let them know that you could have done things differently. Apologize honestly and show them what it looks like to have flaws. In doing so, you not only teach them that imperfect parenting can happen, but also that you can take responsibility for your actions.

Apologize
Luke Van Antwerp

Luke Van Antwerp is a colonel in the US Army and a Special Operations veteran. His father, whom he talks about below, is Lieutenant General (Ret.) Robert L. Van Antwerp Jr., former commanding general of the US Army Corps of Engineers.

One day when I was a kid, my dad apologized for something he had done. *Wow, he made a mistake,* I thought. And here I saw my dad as perfect; I thought he could do no wrong. His apology really made an impact on me, and it was a great reminder that we are all fallible. It taught me that when you do something that requires an apology, you apologize. That goes for soldiers, too. And I try to instill that in my team. If you are unable to apologize, you will never be a great leader.

Let yourself be human in front of your kids. If you spill the milk, laugh about it. If you argue with a friend on the phone in front of them, talk about how friendships are hard and explain that you don't always get it right. If you've missed an important business meeting, talk to your kids about how you'll make it right, and show them what steps you'll take to ensure you follow through. And when the *shit* hits the proverbial fan, demonstrate a positive attitude and keep your cool. Almost every week, you are likely to face some unforeseen challenges; you can either let them get you down or move through them skillfully. Each occurrence is an opportunity to model the right attitude and behavior for your kids. Each life challenge is a real-world teaching moment.

5. MODELING THE "REFRAME"

As a wrestling coach, Jay Jackson had one steadfast rule for his team: if the match goes into overtime, you have to get excited about it. Don't look at it as "Oh, no," but "Oh, yes!" Reframe a seeming negative into a positive. When you are presented with an obstacle, see it as an opportunity rather than a burden. This is what Dr. L does with her clients all the time. It's a common tool used in therapy and coaching practices. When you go to therapy, much of what is done is reframing. "A simple change in voice tone can do the trick," Dr. L says. "'Why did this happen to me?'—sad face, mopey tone, victim mentality—can easily be replaced with curiosity or interest. 'Why *did* this happen to you?'—voice goes up, interested face, curiosity driving the conversation. Doing this with your kids is so valuable because we all understand the power of negativity bias, our tendency to zoom in on the negative, and if we can help them focus on the positives or the opportunity, it's a win."

A NOTE ABOUT COMPARISON

Dr. L reports that one of the most common questions she gets from parents is "Are we doing enough?" Parents are often operating from a position of "not enough" because they compare themselves to other parents. They begin to think more is better, which leads them to overparent, overschedule, overmanage, and overcommit. This feeling of "not enough" is common. We all have it to some degree or another. But it has become much more pervasive lately among the parenting community.

When parents begin comparing their own parenting style and their kids' achievements to those of others, they play a dangerous game. If they compare and feel like they are falling short, they react and do more—scheduling their kids for additional activities, involving themselves where they aren't necessarily needed, or stressing the need for additional achievement in their children. They may also buy more, flooding their children with what other kids have just to ensure they aren't missing out. Those who compare and feel they've come out on top tell themselves they need to stay on top. All of this results in exhausted parents and overtired, overworked, and achievement-focused children.

Remember, we all have different parenting styles, strengths, and weaknesses. And our children have different styles, strengths, and weaknesses, too. Who cares if Mary from down the street plays both soccer and basketball but your child is only participating in dance class? And who cares if Neil from around the block is reading at a third-grade level and your child can't recognize the alphabet yet? So what if Tony has three pairs of Nike sneakers but your child only has one? Stop comparing and start focusing on being the best parent for *your* child, not for the kid down the street. What do you love to do? Share your passion with your child, and it will be more special than anything you feel compelled to do to keep up with the neighbors.

The Gift of Getting Up Early

As you know, one thing I really want to model for my kids is being an early riser. Usually, we work out at home in the earliest hours of the day, but sometimes we mix it up and have adventures. You can get a lot of living done before 9 a.m.

One morning, soon after we had moved to Vancouver, I barged into my kids' rooms as the clock struck 5:30. "Let's go," I said. "I've got a surprise for you." They seemed unimpressed. "Put on your wetsuits," I added. Their ears perked up. Fueled by intrigue, they threw off their covers and quickly got dressed. Of course, when I told them we'd be running to our destination, intrigue turned to apprehension.

"Uh, we're gonna run there? Where to?" they moaned.

"Just follow me," I said.

Off we went, running toward the beautiful beaches of North Vancouver. Twenty minutes into our run, the path in front of us began to slowly open up, and our strides became more labored as we approached the bay. Finally, we reached our finish line for the morning, right where the tide hits the sand along Deep Cove. In the distance, enormous green rocks jutted straight out of the water. Except for our panting, everything was quiet and still.

"Who's that?" my kids asked, motioning to a man walking toward us and grinning widely.

"That's our tour guide," I told them.

Simon Whitfield was the ten-time triathlon world champion and gold medal winner at the 2000 Spartan Summer Games. I had met Simon briefly years earlier, but as soon as we moved to Vancouver, he reached out and insisted I bring the kids out to Deep Cove for the day.

After quick introductions, we each grabbed a paddleboard and waded out into the blue waters. Simon led the way, gliding effortlessly into the unknown. The farther we paddled, the quieter it became. Occasionally, we'd hear a splash as a pink salmon jumped from the water or a seal popped its head out to watch us on our journey. It was just us, the water, and nature as one.

Simon began to quote authors as the sun rose, sharing poetic passages about nature and Mother Earth from writers like Steinbeck and Thoreau. He asked us to name the one book we would each bring if we were trapped on a deserted island. The kids and I debated our favorite writers and themes, struggling to pick just one.

Eventually, we began to make our way back to shore, taking our time and reflecting on the conversation and sights of the morning. There was something so calming and meditative about just the five of us together, moving our arms to the rhythm of the waves. For my kids, this morning adventure was another reward for doing the hard thing, for getting up early, while most of their friends were still sleeping in bed.

Not every early-morning rise is going to be as fun as that one, but my kids are learning that getting up early gives them a jump start on the day. And doing something hard first thing in the morning makes the rest of the day seem a bit easier, no matter what they face.

Give early morning adventures a try with your family. Here's what I suggest:

- Plan something fun for your family to do as a tribe. It could be a hike, an early morning trip to the beach, a canoe trip, fishing, or a ball game, for example.
- Don't tip them off. Make it a surprise.
- Have the car packed and gassed up if needed.
- Set your alarm for 4 a.m. so you can get them up by at least 5.
- Get 'em up. Tell them they have ten minutes to get dressed. You've got a surprise. Let the anticipation motivate movement.
- Go. Have fun. They will complain at first, but they will also find the dark cool of an early-morning adventure exhilarating and memorable. Give them a memory, and they will know they are loved.

In Conclusion

There you have it. Now you know how to dedicate yourself to your daily routine, and you've learned five ways to be a role model, all contingent on being present and engaged when you can. If you can remember that your kids are watching all the time, it becomes easier to show them right from wrong and to give them the tools they will need to be healthy, adaptable, grateful, hardworking, disciplined, kind, and in control. You will always be their most important role model, so be the best you can. And listen, if you're off to a rocky start—which is 100 percent likely to happen with any new routine—keep going. Remember how those bullshit excuses can get in the way? So can bullshit adult tantrums: "I didn't do it well, so I'm just not cut out for it." Stop, take a deep breath, and reboot. These rules for resilience are tough, and they're meant to be. Your kids *will* complain when you start a new morning routine, but that's okay. Keep at it. The minute you let up and they hear you say, "Maybe we shouldn't do this anymore," they'll latch on to that idea like a leech! Trust the process, keep going, and stay the course.

Remember, your routine is yours to discover and uncover. What works for me may not work for you and your family. You've got to connect your routine to your value system. You can't just follow what someone else does and expect it to click like magic. Do whatever works for you, but the important part is to take action. Don't let planning the plan become the bullshit that gets in the way of your executing it. We all know people who buy planners because they believe it'll be the golden ticket to a more structured routine. They're the same people who buy the complete Nike tracksuit for their first workout. Don't be that person.

Discipline Breeds Responsibility

The Impact of Integrity

> Some people regard discipline as a chore. For me, it's an
> order which sets me free to fly.

—Julie Andrews

When my wife was eight and a half months pregnant with our first child, I was still running around doing ultra-marathons, Ironman competitions, and races all over the world. I was training for twelve hours straight every Saturday, in addition to my weekly cross-training workouts. Despite a growing human inside her belly, Courtney was still my number one fan—she was always there, cheering for me and ready to celebrate at the finish line. She's the best spectator any event can have, and it's still one of her favorite things about going to Spartan races. But I had been traveling a ton for work and also for my own races, and shit was about to hit the fan.

I remember one time I flew to South Africa to knock out an Ironman. I landed on a Friday afternoon, put my bike together, woke up the next morning, did the Ironman. At the finish line, I took my bike apart, put it in a box, and got on a plane to go back to New York. When I woke up the next morning, I worked three days on Wall Street, and then flew to Western Australia for another race. I had zero recovery planned into my schedule, and this was just my mindset at the time: keep going no matter what. I was developing the self-discipline I needed to tackle my training, and I'd tapped into something hungry inside me for the first time.

It was a deeply fulfilling time in my life because I'd just gone through a personal transformation: from being chained to my desk job on Wall Street to discovering fitness and training. I was really fired up about health and personal growth, and I wanted to achieve, achieve, achieve.

One day I got home from a marathon, and I was just exhausted. I walked in the door and set my bag down, fully prepared to go straight to bed and let my body sleep off the hell of the previous couple of days. Courtney was standing in the doorway. I'll never forget the look on her face because it is the most loving kick-in-the-ass look I'll ever get.

She said, "Joe, are we going to have a family, or are you just going to keep doing races forever?"

For years, I had been wrestling with the substance beneath the surface of that simple question.

From the moment I found out my wife was pregnant, I was thrilled. I knew that I wanted to be a dedicated, committed father. That had been a longtime goal of mine. However, I didn't know how, or where, to start. When I look back now, I realize that I was giving so much of my time and energy to racing during this season of my life because it had rules, structure, and an end result that I always felt better than when I started. There was clarity to my effort—you put time into training; you work on speed, strength, and endurance; you accomplish this and this and then this; and then you go out and compete and see how strong you are.

Fatherhood wasn't going to come with a set of rules. It would be messy. My efforts might not reap obvious and immediate rewards. I knew how to be disciplined when it came to training for races. I knew I could be disciplined in my job. But as my wife said in her very honest and direct way, When would all this time, energy, and discipline be refocused toward the family we were about to build? Eventually, I had to ask myself, *What am I running from? More important, what should I be running toward?*

You could say that Spartan may have been seeded from my desire to keep the *crazy* of younger Joe and endurance races alive while adding my new role as a father into the mix. I didn't want to walk away from all the ultramarathons, wild adventures, and gnarly races that made me feel incredible and allowed me to do unbelievable things, but I had to change. Courtney made that clear. I couldn't be a great business entrepreneur, an amazing husband and dad, and train for these super-tough races every week. The training alone took me away both Saturday and Sunday. How on earth was that sustainable? It wasn't. I had to cut back on what I wanted to do but creatively devise a plan to keep my love for that world alive. Spartan was the answer.

The point of this story is that at a pivotal moment in life, my wife forced me to take a look in the mirror and decide who I wanted to be. I had become a master at self-discipline and could be disciplined in the most obvious ways—running, lifting, and training; eating incredibly nutritious food; committing myself to the work of preparing for serious competition. But discipline without integrity, responsibility, and service is like letting your ego run wild. That's why whenever I teach discipline, and when I work to access it myself, I do so with character goals in mind.

Discipline and Integrity

The point of reading a book like this one and building true resilience is connecting who you are with your potential. During all of the crazy adventures of my past—climbing mountains, running races, doing Ironman competitions—I gained more than just muscle and endurance and even more than resilience and grit. When you learn how to execute all your plans and how to stop getting in your own way, the world opens up. Through this discipline, I learned the power of integrity.

Integrity works like a structural engineer who walks around a work site and tests the strength of materials. The engineer looks at the foundation and asks, Is it level? Is it sturdy? Can the materials and the structure hold up to outside forces like extreme weather? Can they hold up to everyday wear and tear? How can we make this or that part of the structure stronger in some way? Where can this structure be improved? When my choices are tested, my character challenged, and my values put on the line, it is integrity that keeps me above the fray. Everyday life presents you with a constant stream of resistance—fires at work, kids that are having a hard time, training schedules gone haywire—but you can't go wrong if your integrity is leading the way.

When I was training and going through extreme adversity in ultramarathons and triathlons, I was testing the integrity of my parts—my dependability, reliability, wholeness. And I think when you've suffered the way that I've suffered, *voluntarily* suffered the way that I've suffered, it knocks the edges off and refines you. There's so much to be learned about yourself from those struggles. You learn where you're lacking and what needs work.

But you can also hide behind all of that adversity without extracting the essential lessons. You can run from your life through the sheer mania of work or sports or training or side projects and the discipline you give to them. One reason why I enjoyed races so much at this time in my life was that I was stressed out with my career on Wall Street; when I got to a race, it was a relief to worry about nothing more than the basics: water, food, and shelter. I've met more people like this than you might imagine. They use the tough stuff, the wild adventures and big challenges, to avoid confronting the real issues of their lives. They dedicate themselves to weekly excursions to avoid problems at home. They push themselves to feel tremendous pain in ultramarathons to hide from the grief of losing a loved one. The endorphins and feel-good chemicals from doing the hard shit can be a fantastic barrier to really dealing with life. Make sure you do a gut check with yourself. Are you using adversity as a shield or a savior? And is the structure of who you are capable of handling *all* storms— not just the ones that you choose to test yourself in?

The good news is that discipline allows us to meet ourselves. Discipline enforces a much-needed integrity check. When Courtney and I were expecting our first child, I needed to find out who I was. I had learned to handle situations within the simple framework of an Ironman competition, but how would I handle more complex situations in the other parts of my life? Was the structure of Joe De Sena resilient enough to thrive in the ultramarathon of parenthood?

Discipline and Confidence

Through discipline we also begin to build one of the most important elements of being a healthy human: confidence. There's a common thread present in those who come to my farm to change their life and stop unhealthy habits. A massive lack of confidence. For many, their undisciplined life and out-of-control choices have slowly chipped away at any sense of self-esteem. When they begin to implement structure, routine, and the scaffolding for discipline, their confidence grows. Every time their alarm goes off and they don't hit the snooze button or they complete their chores or get up the mountain without taking a break, it's like an IV drip of self-esteem. As you become more disciplined, you gather more confidence.

One of the best parts of watching new Spartan racers cross the finish line is watching that huge grin of newly built confidence spread across their face. We have a saying at Spartan: "You'll know at the finish line." You'll have to race a race to really know what it means, but let's just say that the discipline it takes to complete such a difficult endeavor gives you an opportunity to meet a part of you that you may not have realized existed. A more confident part. And this contributes to that true resilience we've been talking about.

The thing about true resilience is that it comes quietly, as does the confidence alongside it. Confidence is never the loudest, most talkative, abrasive energy in the room. It's the quiet, contained person in the corner who doesn't need to suck up all the oxygen. When I meet a really tough wrestler or Navy SEAL or Delta Force operator, I always expect some demonstration of power in their handshake, but it's often very measured. They've been through some tough shit, and the way they wear it is in the form of humility and openness. When you've been broken and rebuilt, you don't need to prove anything to anyone. You know yourself.

My wife admires people who are humble and have a quiet confidence, people who are completely capable and talented and don't need to tell the world. She reminds the kids, "You don't need to rev a Ferrari. If you're sitting at a traffic light and someone is driving a Ferrari, everyone knows it. There is no need to rev your engine and be a show-off. The Ferrari just needs to *be* a Ferrari. Just own it and be humble."

Making a Mark on the World

In his bestselling book *Discipline Equals Freedom*, retired Navy SEAL commander Jocko Willink writes, "Self-discipline, as the very term implies, comes from the SELF. . . . When you make a decision to do more, to BE more, self-discipline comes when you decide to make a mark on the world."

That's powerful stuff. Most people think of discipline all wrong. They think it is going to give them something they desperately want, like a promotion or a weight loss photo to post on Instagram. For them, it's a means to an end. Sure, you might end up with some wins once you decide to get disciplined in working toward a goal. But the gift of discipline is really the service it provides others. When you are disciplined with your time, efforts, and self, you can clear away the bullshit and make a real impact through focus and hard work. Making a mark on the world needs to be your *why* for embracing self-discipline.

I can't say this often enough: the world needs you at your best. We need all of your skills to help analyze problems and create solutions. Why do you want to run that marathon or lose those last ten pounds or quit drinking? If the answer isn't about making a mark on the world in some way, then the discipline to follow through won't follow. Or if it does, it will be a lonely and self-seeking and ultimately unfulfilling road toward your goal.

Connecting the idea of making your mark on the world with discipline is most obvious when we look at the Greatest Generation, those who lived, worked, and served the country through the Second World War.

Let me set a scene for you. The year is 1945. A troop transporter steams into New York Harbor and offloads thousands of American GIs, many of whom were just boys when they enlisted. You ask one nineteen-year-old about the hardest thing he's ever done. What demanded the most mental toughness? If he hesitates, it's because he's weighing his options: hypothermia, trench foot, seeing a buddy get shot, killing an enemy soldier. He has lived a whole life in his brief time at war. His twin sister could tell you about making bullets and breaking Nazi codes. She sacrificed her youth for the war effort, too. But what they gained through those tough times was a steely mental toughness and remarkable perseverance that would serve the Greatest Generation well as they built the nation we know today.

In his book *The Greatest Generation*, the legendary journalist Tom Brokaw makes the case that the men and women who came of age during World War II developed the values of "personal responsibility, duty, honor, and faith" and a work ethic that propelled the American economy forward and created historic advances in science and social programs. He calls them "achievements of a magnitude the world had never before witnessed." Brokaw was one of those men. Lauded as one of the best journalists in the world, he demonstrated an unwavering commitment to telling other people's stories, and he left his own mark on the world.

I think about the Greatest Generation often when trying to align my daily discipline with how I want to leave my mark. Disciplined people can make the world better. That's critical to remember. The schedule you're sticking to and the effort you're putting in is helping others. You have no idea how many people are affected by your decision to show up and give your best effort without complaint.

Here's the good news: surviving a war isn't the only path to building honor, integrity, and a sense of duty in your life. The trick is to come up with a *why* (flip back to rule 4, Live Your Values, if you need some inspiration), and then do what I do: remind yourself of the struggle and sacrifice of other people.

Whenever I'm finding it tough to get disciplined or persevere, I think of someone who has it harder than I do. And then I say their name out loud, picturing them in my mind. I think of that guy stuck in solitary confinement for a crime he didn't commit. Or a veteran with a missing limb who shows up to training sessions with a smile. That allows me to suddenly see my world in a new way. What a gift it is to have two arms. What a gift it is to be free in my house surrounded by family.

My advice is to come up with a go-to person to call to mind, someone you can reference when the going gets tough, when you don't want to do those last ten burpees. You can think of them and remember that your sacrifice is nothing compared to theirs. Together, those sacrifices make the world a better place for everyone.

Work Ethic

Employers today are seeing early signs of a generational shift in discipline among their workers. They claim that current generations of workers have a less developed work ethic than previous generations. Researchers engaged in a Center for Creative Leadership study of the current workforce, "Problem Employees," surveyed and interviewed managers in a broad range of occupations, asking them to describe common negative employee behaviors. These were the top complaints:

> Failure to meet minimum requirements
> Failure to assume responsibility
> Lack of respect
> Low job commitment
> Poor teamwork
> Negative attitude

Wow. When I look at this list, I wonder what we're doing *right*. In most of the research on work ethic and the modern workforce, hiring managers described millennials—even those with college degrees—as being unprepared for the job market and lacking an adequate work ethic. So what happened with millennials?

The truth is that I feel for younger millennials for two reasons. First, they're being sold a bill of goods; they're told that their work ethic should first and foremost be geared toward their purpose and that they should find what they love and get paid for doing it. Well, wouldn't that be grand! In an ideal world, we would *all* find what we love and get paid for it, but this is not that world. We need to manage expectations here. It's not impossible for this age cohort to find the perfect combo of purpose + paycheck, but it is rather rare. Remember, purpose or passion can come from outside the workplace. You can do your job and then engage in what you love to do when you get home. Or you can use the morning hours to hone your craft before beginning your commute to that 9 to 5. It's a luxury to be able to combine your purpose with your income, not a birthright.

When I started my pool business way back when, it wasn't because the sparkling pools fed my soul and the leaf skimmer filled my spiritual cup. It was because I wanted to make money, plain and simple. The same can be said for my work on Wall Street. It wasn't my passion; it was a means to an end. I worked for my paycheck and I found my passion elsewhere—on one-hundred-mile adventure runs and Ironman challenges. Helping to transform lives through Spartan is my purpose—of that I'm sure—but the idea that everyone will feel passionate about their work is misguided.

Second, let's remember that millennials have benefited from many innovations that make their world substantially more comfy than that of previous generations. Immediate gratification from Instagram likes, next-day or same-day delivery, and algorithmically recommended Netflix shows have set millennials up to believe that things should come easily and be delivered at a moment's notice, that success can just be handed over. Unfortunately, this perceived template for how the world works will not translate to an immediate seat in the C-suite. Here's a simple example. Remember the busy signal? When you called someone and they were on the other line, all you heard was *beep, beep, beep, beep*. It was annoying, but there was no alternative, so you just managed. You hung up the phone, did something else, and then tried again a few minutes later. You learned that you couldn't have immediate access to what (or whom) you wanted. Millennials didn't grow up with a busy signal. They grew up with call waiting and cell phones—where everyone was accessible, and immediate gratification was common. It's no wonder that this group has a difficult time understanding that real success is built from real work.

How Do You Build Work Ethic?

Work ethic is a set of values based on consistency and diligence. Your work ethic is closely tied to your character. It's a part of you. Work ethic is the internalized acceptance that struggle is to be expected and that doing the task at hand without complaining is morally right. It's about taking responsibility, sacrificing for a greater good, and having pride in a job completed skillfully. When I think of work ethic, I think of our parents and grandparents—the Greatest Generation—and their stoic resolve amid the challenges and uncertainty of World War II. I also think of the origin story of Chief Warrant Officer 3 Joe Nye, who retired after thirty years of service in the army. He writes:

> My parents were both raised in the height of the depression and it was especially tough on my father, since his father left home a little after his brother was born, leaving my grandmother with three young kids in the house. When I was eight my dad retired from the Air Force and then proceeded to

work a series of jobs, often two at a time. For most of my life, my memory is of my Dad working a morning shift and then a bartending shift at the Newark Country Club until 11:30 at night. (I know this because as a teenager if I wanted to use the car, I had to take him to work at 4:00 p.m. and then pick him up at 11:30 p.m.) At different times in my life, Dad and I shared the same job, picking potatoes for extra money in Maine, delivering *Philadelphia Inquirer* newspapers in Delaware, selling Charles Chips potato chips door to door, and working at an auto auction together. Whatever he was doing, he worked hard at it, whether it was at the job site, doing yard work, or cooking dinner. He gave everything his all. He also reminded us that during his childhood, he gave every penny he ever made to his mother to help out. So, as a kid, if I wanted any money, I had to make it myself; we were not an allowance family. I was a paperboy early on, I sold greeting cards door to door. For as far back as I can remember, I had a job because my father taught me the value of a dollar and the work ethic that's required to get it.

You can't take the *work* out of *work ethic*. You might have all the good intentions in the world, but if you don't put those intentions into action, they are useless. You must get to work to build work ethic. Be like Officer Nye's father. Take that night shift if it means more money and stability for your family, more discipline in every other area of life, and greater personal integrity when you think about a job well done. Remember that there is no room for ego in work ethic. Work ethic sprouts from work in every form, from selling potato chips to delivering newspapers. The more you work, the greater your work ethic.

Humans Crave Discipline

We don't like to admit it, but we are a species that craves discipline. This is true of us, our kids, and those we lead in our immediate and extended family, at work, and beyond. Humans are creatures of discipline. We *want* to be accountable and work hard.

Why, then, are we so weak and so resistant to hard, gritty work? Opting out is a powerful opponent. We have to actively fight against our instinct to quit. That fight is only won if we can honor our craving for discipline. When you hear that alarm go off in the morning but your head is foggy and you want to roll over and hit snooze, you have to fight that weakness in yourself. When you are on your eleventh rep of twelve and everything is burning, you have to fight that weakness in yourself. When you are faced with a possible confrontation and you want to lie or evade your way out of it instead of telling the truth and having integrity, you have to fight that weakness in yourself. How? By trusting that you have more to give and that your contribution to the world matters. It's easy to quit if you believe that nobody gives a shit. So remind yourself daily that your mark on the world is important. Whether it's serving food to others, stacking books at the bookstore, developing new medical devices, or cleaning the bathrooms at the elementary school—all of it *matters*.

Discipline Breeds Responsibility: For the Family

Kids learn responsibility and a strong work ethic by seeing it in their parents, family members, and other adults in their lives. Do you notice a theme? If kids don't have role models, it can be very difficult for them to learn these traits.

In 2017, my family and I were living in Japan to grow Spartan's business in Asia. I had a friend over there who introduced us to the new neighborhood, and I saw his wife at the bus stop one day. She was polite and perfectly dressed, and she nodded to me as we waited for the bus. Because she didn't speak English and I was far from fluent in Japanese, we couldn't really communicate. Soon her son got off the bus, and though I couldn't understand all she said, I understood that she told him it was time to go to Kumon, a math program that originated in our Japanese neighborhood. Well, this kid threw a fit, screaming, kicking, and getting his mom's perfect clothes all dirty. It was shocking. Where I come from, you don't disrespect your mom like that. I grabbed the kid and gave him a bear hug, showing him that someone was there who wouldn't tolerate that lack of discipline. He thrashed a bit but calmed down.

Then he walked like a soldier with his mom to Kumon.

Every time I saw that kid after that, he saluted me and smiled. He wanted my respect. His father and mother were amazed. The kid had never been properly disciplined before.

Kids want discipline, which is a type of boundary that provides direction, and they thrive when they get it. I got more chances to see this kid grow emotionally and physically. His mom introduced my kids to a Japanese wrestling program based in the samurai tradition, and our families went together. Much ritual was built into the wrestling program, and that's exactly what discipline is: ritually following through on small tasks until you can accomplish the "impossible" project. That's why every ancient tradition, whether it's from the Spartans or the samurai, begins with rituals of discipline. In the Japanese wrestling school, the kids would set up the mats before we started, and then the moms and kids would take washcloths and buff them with beautiful motions. The kids were required to do this chore to be part of the team. The coach would start with a fifteen-minute prayer, a tradition that had been carried on for centuries. These rituals, these acts of being accountable to the whole group, gave the kids a sense of pride and belonging.

When you impose daily chores on your children, like making the bed every day or unloading the dishwasher, and hold them accountable, it will instill a sense of responsibility and belonging to the family. When you teach children to power through the pain and failure of attempting a chin-up over and over, eventually they will get their chin above the bar, but it happens in small increments. It's not easy, but you have to push your kids hard. External discipline eventually goes inside children and becomes self-discipline. Remember that we're raising future adults, and we want those adults to be responsible and considerate friends, partners, and workers. Here are a few strategies to implement at home and in the family to grow the kind of discipline that breeds responsibility.

SET BOUNDARIES

The concept of setting boundaries is simple, but the implementation of boundary enforcement is complicated. Setting a boundary is a simple way of identifying what's okay and what is not okay. It's like an invisible line that you draw around yourself to say, "This is mine, and that is yours," or, "This behavior is okay, and that is not." Boundaries are essential in families because they give kids a guidebook explaining the rules.

But let's be honest: kids push boundaries. It's actually a healthy part of development. It can wear on us over time, but it's only natural. You've been there: your toddler reaches for more raisins after you've told him no, your twelve-year-old rolls her eyes when you call her name, or you find your teenager wearing one of your shirts without asking. There are lots of creative ways that kids can push and cross boundaries.

Many parents are afraid to set boundaries or to address the issue when boundaries have been crossed because they are worried about upsetting their children. So instead they placate and pander, let the boundary become muddy, and refrain from standing firm. The result is an entitled child who doesn't have a firm sense of self. Dr. L says that this is always a source of contention when she works with parents. "You have to be able to set boundaries and then maintain them. Oftentimes parents will say something like, 'Well, sure, he came home after curfew, but if we make a big deal out of it, he'll get so angry and freak out. Better to just let it be.' No. No. It's not better. What your child is learning when you don't enforce boundaries is, *I can do what I want without consequence.* Fast-forward two years and they get kicked off the basketball team for missing practice, five years and they fail a course in college because they didn't show up, and ten years and they lose their dream job because they can't get to work on time. You might be avoiding a nightmare tantrum in the present, but you're creating a much bigger problem in the future."

Boundaries are key for developing a true sense of self. There must be a clear line separating your children from you. Kids are kids, not parents. Boundaries help remind them of that present reality. Remember, their brains are not as developed as ours. They can't undergo the type of thoughtful decision-making process that we can, so letting them set the rules is a dangerous choice.

Be clear and firm when setting your boundaries. A secure and stable household comes with firm, consistent boundaries. Let them know what is okay and what is not okay. Stop equating the word *boundary* with punishment or authoritarianism. Boundaries are gifts you give your kids.

START EARLY

The best time to start teaching your kids about personal responsibility and the value of a strong work ethic is the moment you realize they can pick up their toys. Can your kids pick up a ball, a blankie, or a pacifier? Good. Put them to work picking up toys and putting them away. The same goes for clothes. Once your kids can pick up a piece of clothing, there are only three options: hang it up, fold it and put it in a drawer, or toss it in the laundry. With most kids, you can start this kind of chore training as early as age two. If you don't, prepare to trip over their toys when they are six and wade through piles of sweatshirts and sneakers when they are twelve.

Consider most teenagers. Compared to the adults they live with, many teenagers contribute little to the cleanliness and order of the household. Why? Perhaps their parents never made them put their toys away or make their bed or fix themselves a snack when they were younger. The parents did it all for them. So now the parents are eternally relegated to the roles of housekeeper, chef, and chief nag. Can you see how the pattern develops? When parents do everything for their kids from an early age, they are more likely to continue doing everything for the kids when they are eighteen.

In addition, if you pick up your children's toys, you'll be sending a clear message that they are not capable. How sad is that? Give your kids the credit they deserve. If you give your kids responsibilities and duties, not only will they learn that they are capable but they'll experience the power of hard work.

Most kids *want* to help. They want to be like mom and dad, mimicking the things you do. Use that desire to your advantage. Give them responsibilities as soon as they can walk, and keep it up through elementary school, middle school, and high school, increasing the amount of responsibility as they age. You'll be training them to be capable, independent adults—with neatly made beds and organized garages. And guess what? In time, they'll teach your grandchildren not to leave their toys on the floor. You won't trip and break your hip, and all will be right with the world.

In addition to teaching your kids to be responsible for their own stuff, what's the best way to teach responsibility and instill a strong work ethic in your kids? Show, don't tell. Model responsibility and a strong work ethic in your own life.

BUILD DISCIPLINE AROUND FEELINGS

We've all done it in a moment of weakness. We're at the store and our toddler suddenly becomes a wailing rag doll, throwing a tantrum on the floor because he wants a toy we refused to buy. So we cave and buy the toy just to shush him up and avoid the judgmental eyes of our fellow shoppers. As far as shopping survival strategies go, it may not seem like such a big deal. It's not, really, unless it becomes a pattern that carries into the elementary school years, the preteen years, or, heaven forbid, the teenage years. By that time, you may have dug a hole that you cannot dig your family out of.

I call this pattern the "happiness hoax." People-pleasing parents work harder and harder to ensure their kids are "happy." They think this is the right way to raise pleasant, optimistic, and well-adjusted children. If their child grows up to be a "happy person," then they've succeeded as a parent. But it's a big misstep. First, they've conflated *well-adjusted* and *happy*. We all know that being well-adjusted sometimes has nothing to do with being happy. Being well-adjusted is about adaptability—being able to flex when things become rough—and adjusting to circumstances that are out of your control. None of that includes the word *happy*.

In the vigilant pursuit of moment-to-moment happiness,

parents are not allowing their kids to build the life skill of distress tolerance. As a result, these children become intolerant of any painful or difficult feelings, including boredom, irritation, anger, sadness, and disappointment. They can't handle the ebbs and flows of life, let alone the tough stuff, and sometimes this can lead to more serious mental health issues. That's why we as parents have to appreciate it when our kids display a completely appropriate emotional response, even if it's difficult for us to see. Let's say your child doesn't get picked for the A team in soccer despite much practice and hard work. What would a normal emotion be following this news? That's right, disappointment. When you as their parent swoop in at that moment to alleviate your kid's disappointment with a tub of ice cream or a trip to Target to buy the newest video game, you send them two important but destructive messages: first, that a painful feeling should immediately be attended to and transformed into comfort, and second, that we can alleviate painful feelings with food, purchases, or anything else that you may have brought into the mix. Fast-forward twenty years, and now you've got a thirty-year-old who can't tolerate disappointment and uses ice cream or spending to alleviate the emotion.

Dr. L often encounters this unhealthy pattern. "Oftentimes, the adults who arrive in my office have deep-rooted associations and playbooks for how the world works, and these were fused early on in life," she says. "They had parents who bought them more toys when their favorite one broke, made alternative meals if they complained about what was set on their dinner plate, intervened with coaches if they weren't put in the starting lineup, and would stage second Christmas mornings if the first one didn't make their child happy enough. The primary lesson that is often learned is that anything outside of happy is to be fixed immediately. The adult sitting in my office is struggling with life's heartache because they haven't had any experience."

Kids can learn to rely on everything being handed to them by parents who simply want them to be happy. These kids may never learn how to work for something themselves. Saying no to your child may be the best defense against this entitlement, laziness, and *real* maladjustment. Some of the most challenging obstacles that any of us have to face are our own feelings. Fear, grief, anger, shame, disappointment—none of these are a walk in the park. For me, a rope climb feels far easier to handle than the disappointment I have in a team member who lets me down. Remind yourself and your kids that emotions can be obstacles, too, but with practice and discipline we can learn to manage the hard feelings.

A rising generation of Americans who work hard and don't act entitled is built one child at a time. There is a lot you can do yourself to foster responsibility, self-discipline, and a strong work ethic in your kids. There's no set formula. Much of your success will depend on your ability to discern what sparks enthusiasm and motivation in your child. So, let's start there.

Here are six things that you can do to teach responsibility and work ethic at home.

1 *Find your kid's flow.* The easiest ways to establish a solid work ethic in children is to find out what they're passionate about and give them every opportunity to get lost in pursuing it. Are you familiar with the work of the Hungarian American psycho-

analyst Mihaly Csikszentmihalyi? The mind doc wrote a popular book in the 1990s called *Flow: The Psychology of Optimal Experience*, in which he explored the roots of happiness and its correlation to what he called the "flow state." Csikszentmihalyi (pronounced *cheek-sent-me-high*) found that when people were at their most creative, productive, and satisfied, they were in a state of flow. They became lost in the moment, and their exceptional performance happened without effort—for example, Michael Jordan in his prime on the basketball court with the Chicago Bulls or Mia Hamm making every soccer goal look so easy for Team USA.

Think of a time when your children were so wrapped up in whatever they were doing that they lost all track of time. And no, we're not talking about the trance of video games here. Remember when your kids got totally involved in building a Lego castle or were so focused that they just had to finish writing a few more sentences of their story or chose not to play tag with the kids on the block but instead meticulously and effortlessly worked on their basketball free throws? That's a glimpse into flow. If you can identify that type of passion in your children, you can use it to build a powerful work ethic.

2 ***Give them chores and a reason to value them.*** Nobody really loves to do chores, especially children, but that's the point of this critical step in developing discipline. Chores are important because of the many ways they benefit child development:

- Chores teach responsibility and self-reliance.
- Chores teach planning and time-management skills.
- Chores help kids develop pride in their achievements; they will feel the success of a job done well.
- Chores reinforce respect and value. If your child sweeps the floor, he or she will be less likely to track mud into the house.
- Chores foster family bonding and demonstrate the value of teamwork.

Need some ideas? Here are a few chores that you can start delegating to your children right now:

- Putting away their own laundry
- Washing the dishes
- Taking the dog for a walk and cleaning up after it
- Taking out the trash
- Shoveling snow off the sidewalk
- Watering the plants
- Vacuuming
- Cleaning their room and making their bed
- Feeding the pets

3 *Put a high price on punctuality.* I learned early that "on time" was late and "early" was on time. Teaching the importance of being on time (early) for every appointment and commitment is an excel-

lent way to establish self-discipline and work ethic. Time management is at the core of a strong work ethic. To be on time, your child must learn how to plan and organize—essential building blocks for discipline. In addition, being on time demonstrates respect for others. When your children show up for their drum lesson or karate class on time, they show respect for the teacher and your hard-earned money. Of course, if you're trying to teach them punctuality, make sure you hold yourself to the same standard. Don't be late dropping them off or picking them up.

4 *Cultivate self-discipline through independence.* Allow your children to follow through with duties, chores, and responsibilities on their own. If you are always jumping in and doing everything for them, or correcting their little mistakes, they will lose motivation and increase dependency. One of the best ways to ensure that this doesn't happen is to allow them to be alone while they are completing a chore. This not only prevents you from impulsively stepping in when they don't do something exactly how you would do it, but it reminds them that you *trust* they can do it on their own. If you're lurking in the background, you're unintentionally fostering that learned helplessness that we talked about earlier. Remember, we're not cultivating perfection here—we're celebrating hard work and discipline. That being said, don't let your kids get away with a shit job. If their chore is to fold the laundry and you encounter what looks like a heaping pile of cot-

ton on their floor, make sure they understand your expectations for a job well done. Effort matters: you don't want your kids putting 5 percent effort into their chores and 95 percent effort into Donkey Kong.

5 *Stress accountability.* If your children forget to complete a school assignment, it is their responsibility to let the teacher know, not yours. It's not helpful for you to write an excuse note. Demonstrate to your children that they are in charge of, and responsible for, their performance at school and in all areas of their life. When you step in to clean up their mess, it teaches them that you'll always be there to fix things. Dr. L says, "Be forward-thinking. You may be dealing with a kid right now, but that kid will eventually grow into an adult. Do you really want to be calling their employer when they're thirty? Or stepping in as a mediator if they are having struggles in their marriage? Probably not, but I've seen it all before. A fifty-five-year-old dad who had lost his father a year earlier said to me in a session, 'My dad always fixed everything. I can't believe I'm this old and have no idea how to do this myself.' Don't be that parent who cleans up every mess."

Even the smallest gestures can be overreaching. If your daughter leaves her sweatshirt at a neighbor's house, don't walk over and grab it. Send your child. If your son leaves the garage door open after playing with friends, don't tap the button because it's "just easier." Call your son down and have him do it himself. Remember, the small gestures matter just as much as the big ones. You've got to be disciplined to ensure that they are taught this essential trait.

6 *Encourage autonomy.* Allow your kids the space and time to make decisions and take actions on their own. This builds what psychologists call "self-agency," which is the ability to understand that you can make your own choices and that you have some sense of control over what comes next. When kids understand that their choices will create consequences for them, it helps them be more thoughtful and intentional. They have to weigh the costs and benefits themselves. As a parent, it's hard to sit back and let them choose, especially when you see what's coming. If, for example, you know that a choice is going to bring emotional distress, it's natural for you to want to correct their course. But remember, the goal is not to shield them from pain and distress. The goal is to teach them that they can tolerate whatever comes their way.

Autonomy also helps kids build self-confidence, even if the choice goes awry. They begin to see themselves as capable and strong. This bodes well for them later in life because it strengthens their decision-making processes. They feel more confident not just in their choice but in their ability to make a decision.

The University of Arkansas created a chart to help parents choose the right activity when assigning duties to their offspring. Here is their list of age-appropriate chores.

- Two- to three-year-olds can put toys away, dress themselves, and help put clean dishes away.
- Four- to five-year-olds can help feed pets, make their beds (maybe not perfectly), and help clear the table after dinner.
- Six- to seven-year-olds can wipe tables and counters, put laundry away, and vacuum floors.
- Eight- to nine-year-olds can load and unload the dishwasher, help prepare meals, and make their own lunch.
- Ten- to eleven-year-olds can change their bedding, clean the kitchen or bathroom, and mow the lawn.
- Children aged twelve and above can wash the car, babysit younger siblings, and help shop for groceries with a list.

A NEW GREATEST GENERATION: THE COVID KIDS

It's impossible to ignore what the COVID pandemic of 2020 took from us: lives, jobs, a sense of security, a stable economy, hugs, and handshakes. I often wonder, *What will my kids remember from this time? How will the pandemic shape the way they see the world? How will it impact how they see themselves?* I know that it's hard to think back on 2020 as anything but a shit show, but the truth is that it offered a lot of potentially life-changing lessons that our kids can learn from and possible opportunities that they can capitalize on.

Think about it—our kids were yanked from school mid-year, isolated at home, unable to see friends or go to the playground or see a movie. For kindergarteners, their first year in school was either not in school at all or experienced behind a plastic dome and a mask, unable to see anyone's facial expressions. For high schoolers, proms were canceled, final sports seasons were ended, scholarships were lost. For freshman college students, their first year away from home . . . wasn't. It was spent at home, staring at a screen, trying to make new friends with names on a computer. Our kids endured a shit ton, and they will undoubtedly be stronger for it—*if* we let them be.

If you consider how much resilience and adaptability some of these kids have built just through mere circumstance, it's phenomenal. But we have to keep it alive. And that starts with not just what you do but how you talk about this time. I challenge you to use language that highlights these skills rather than focuses on how "horrible" 2020 was. Ask your kids to write down all the things that they learned during the pandemic, how they grew, what skills they acquired. You may be surprised, and wouldn't that be amazing?

In Conclusion

As your kids get older, they either will or will not have self-discipline and a strong work ethic and take responsibility for their actions. We all know people on both ends of the spectrum. The choice is yours. If you teach them early to embrace these character traits, you'll give them a leg up in life. If you avoid this tremendous responsibility, you'll watch as they flail in their adult years. One way or another, everyone who makes it in life eventually embraces these behaviors. Why not start early so you never have to stand by and watch them suffer?

The discipline that you choose to show in taking these lessons off the page and into your home will be a good test of the level of hard work you're willing to invest. Although your work as a parent will be difficult, it won't be impossible. You might even want to write down all the areas where you know you might struggle. It's a good exercise in self-awareness, and it will signal to you where you need to pay extra attention. Remember that a strong work ethic is as essential at home as it is at work.

Into the Wild

Find Joy in Exercise and Resist Devices

> If you can fill the unforgiving minute with sixty seconds'
> worth of distance run—
> Yours is the Earth and everything that's in it.
>
> —Rudyard Kipling

When Courtney and I first moved to Vermont in 2004, I completely drank the Kool-Aid. I wanted to leave the fast-paced activity of Wall Street behind and trade it in for a simpler, slower lifestyle. It was a new chapter for us, and though we had no idea what we were doing, we were ready to jump in headfirst.

We purchased a beautiful farm with a classic red barn—the perfect emblem of simplicity. The farmhouse needed some renovation, but there was enough space for us to create our own vision, and the mountain behind the property called my name. I thought, *This is just what I need to slow myself down—a little taste of the simple life.* We had big dreams of an enormous greenhouse where we could grow all our food. We'd have cows to milk, goats and chickens to attend to, and a pitchfork would become my best friend. I wanted to trade in Trader Joe for Farmer Joe.

And then Mother Nature intervened. Everything was harder than I imagined it would be. Vermont's cycle of seasons—from the frigid winters to the hot, humid, mosquito-filled summers—kicked my ass. Courtney and I had lived in Boston just prior to moving up to the woods, so it wasn't as if we weren't used to the seasons changing. But living the crystal cold winter, musty fall, and earthy spring was a whole different story. Our senses were both lifted and tested. We spent hours, days, and weeks trying to get our new farm in order. Our vegetable garden was failing. We had no idea what we were doing with the farm animals that we had purchased. And most of our new neighbors wanted us *gone*. Some of the townspeople were so turned off by big city mice invading their country town that they literally made a sign that read GO HOME JOE. It wasn't exactly the idyllic, out-in-nature farm life that we had imagined.

But true to form, we learned how to make lemonade out of lemons—figuratively and literally. We began appreciating the turnover in seasons, learning how each one brought something hard but also something awesome. With the summer heat came family excursions to the nearby pond, with the icy cold winters came opportunities to test out our snowshoe skills, and with the spring came chances to blaze new trails and set new paths up the mountain. Everything that had made our transition tough could be flipped and seen as something that also made our life there beautiful. Our life in Vermont was a combination of *Gladiator*, *The Money Pit*, *The Shining*, and *Funny Farm*.

The unrelenting power of the outdoors literally changed the course of my life. In fact, our farm was where the idea for both Spartan and the Death Race was born. We may manufacture obstacles for our races, but the toughest obstacles often aren't the ones my team puts together with nuts and bolts but rather the ones that Mother Nature gives us, whether we ask for them or not. Rain, mud, snow, wind, heat, cold, water—it's the earth that presents racers with some of their greatest struggles. And this all came from my experience on the farm, where the weather doesn't give two shits about whether you're prepared.

You'll notice that weather conditions have played a part in a few of my stories. That's because my family spends an enormous amount of time outside, in the elements, getting our nature fix. When we are all at the farm, we hike up the mountain daily, eat lunch on the grass, play soccer in the backyard. We spend as much time outside as possible, and our brains and bodies are better for it.

Resilience is not built in safe spaces. It is forged by interacting with unpredictable forces—like uneven rocks on a path, heavy wind, slippery mud, unforeseen storm clouds. The most resilient people I know—firefighters, soldiers, endurance athletes—have typically spent time working under intense pressure and in precarious situations. To prepare for the unpredictability of a dire circumstance, you have to expose yourself to the most unpredictable environment we know, Mother Nature's world. Ask endurance athletes if they prefer to prepare for big competitions indoors on a treadmill or outside on the trails, and they'll tell you that outdoor conditions always prepare them best.

When the pandemic hit, I heard the horror stories of parents glued to the news and to their phones. Kids couldn't peel themselves away either, and it created a kind of global nervous energy the likes of which I'd never seen before. The information flow wasn't serving us well; it was enslaving us to our screens. In chapter 6 you learned about how dedicating to a daily routine is critical for not succumbing to this kind of crisis mentality. In this chapter I hope to make it clear to you that obsession with technology does more than steal our time, zap our focus, and hijack our attention—it prevents us from enjoying the natural world we were born to embrace and be a part of. You can't build true resilience without nature.

The Nature Solution

One of the most well-known tasks in the adult Death Race is chopping wood. Newcomers will scoff at the chore before they start, whispering about how they thought the race was going to be *hard* and snickering over the menial task. Twenty minutes in, we lose about a quarter of our contestants; after an hour, we've lost over half. You would think that something as primal as chopping wood would be easy, but when you're in it and your forearms are burning so bad you can't possibly imagine lifting the ax again, it's a different story. And this is one of the best things about nature—you don't have to look far if you want to be challenged. Some of the most primal activities can teach you the most essential life lessons. Want an exercise in patience? Try lighting a fire without flint. Want delayed gratification? Try building a shelter that can withstand the rain using only dead branches, and sleep in it during a rainstorm. Need some courage? Have a friend lead you into the woods blindfolded, and try to find your way home. Nature has everything you need to build true resilience; you just have to be willing.

While nature can undoubtedly be an arena in which you find grit and resilience, it can also be one where you find peace and calm. My mom knew that nature was restorative. When she moved my sister and me out of Queens and into Ithaca she was tuned in to the benefits of being outside. She didn't want us confined to the concrete jungle anymore. She longed for big maple and oak trees and sprawling hillsides. And though I wasn't thrilled with the idea, I admit that the change was a welcome adventure.

You might have heard the phrase "nature's medicine," but did you know that nature literally has healing powers? Studies show that even minor exposure to nature can hasten healing. If you ever find yourself in a hospital, ask for a room with a window through which you can see nature. Or just have someone bring you a plant. You'll recover faster and ask for less pain medicine.

When you're out in nature, your brain enters the alpha state—that incredible state where you are relaxed but focused. The Japanese understand the power of nature so well that they engage in a practice called "forest bathing," spending an hour or two in the forest. Forest bathing has been shown to decrease symptoms of depression and anxiety and to increase cardiovascular health. Resilience isn't just about doing hard shit. It's also about knowing where you can recharge and recover, and nature's backyard is the perfect place.

Technology Burnout

It never ceases to amaze me how often parents complain about their kids' devices. My first question is always "So you won't mind, then, if I take your phone and throw it in the river?" The response is usually a nervous laugh and a protective hand over the pocket where the phone is kept. We adults are so obsessed with our technology that we don't even realize we're engaging with it nearly every moment of our waking hours—from email, social media, and Netflix to Apple Watches, GPS navigation systems, and audiobooks.

No wonder your kids think it's fine to grab the video game console the minute school is over. They see you reach for your technological crutch, too.

This is an area where I have a difficult time. I don't scroll through social media or play games, but I use my phone all the time to do work. Emails, texts, business calls—it's all done on my phone, especially when I travel. It's scary how often I grab my phone without even thinking of it. I'll be in the middle of a conversation, and my hand will just automatically pick the darn thing up. I don't even know why. I know I'm no Superman, but if I can fall into the technology trap, anyone can.

A few months into the pandemic, I started to really struggle—all our team meetings were being done via Zoom, all the *Spartan Up!* podcast interviews migrated to mobile, and we went from putting on races to creating massive amounts of digital content. I was in technology overload. I noticed that my mood had started to suffer—I was more irritable, felt sluggish, and had a hard time staying focused during meetings. The same thing was happening to my kids. When they spent even a little extra time on their screens, the next thirty minutes were a nightmare. Snarky comments, saucy attitudes—they didn't even feel like my kids! The antidote to all this? A trip outside. Anytime I started to feel sluggish, I would head outside for a deep breath and hike up the mountain. Even if I had only ten minutes, I'd make the most of it—and yes, I'd always bring the kids. Just being outside would clear our heads and give us a glimpse of the *actual* world.

Many have said that the work-from-home culture that sprang up during the pandemic had its benefits, but from my perspective those were far outnumbered by the drawbacks. The biggest disadvantage was that we became even more obsessed with and hyperconnected to our technology than ever before. Workdays were no longer bounded by the morning commute and evening drive home, making it difficult to know when the day started and ended. It all led back to technology. Sleep was disrupted, effective communication became difficult, and productivity suffered.

So how do we get out of this? Put down the screens, breathe some fresh air, and move your body.

The Best Gym Is the Natural World

Richard Louv, author of *Last Child in the Woods* and originator of the term *nature-deficit disorder*, writes, "As the young spend less of their lives in natural surroundings, their senses narrow, physiologically and psychologically, and this reduces the richness of human experience. . . . At the very moment that the bond is breaking between the young and the natural world, a growing body of research links our physical, mental, and spiritual health directly to our association with nature."

Human beings are very much a product of our evolution on earth. The sound of running water steadies us. The fresh air braces us. The sunshine cheers us. The cold wakes us. The raw elements challenge us. Nature acts on human beings in ways we're only beginning to understand. The wilderness lives inside of us, inside every cell, even as we spend more and more of our time indoors and in the virtual world. When we separate ourselves from the natural world that produced us, our senses dull, our attention fragments, and we become more susceptible to anxiety and depression. Many studies have shown that children who stare at a screen too much of the day can become nearsighted, losing the ability to see into the distance, which is what made early human beings such effective hunters and gatherers. When we stop living in the natural world, we literally lose our senses, from the ability to feel our bodies in space to the ability to identify scents and see distances. This is the reason we set Spartan races in some of the most spectacular natural environments in the world, from the desserts of Abu Dhabi to the dazzling beauty of the Colorado Rockies to the lushness of Kualoa Ranch in Oahu, Hawaii. We want you to get outside and experience this glorious planet with all of your senses.

Why Exercise Matters

There's another reason I love being outside, and it goes beyond the hard stuff, nature's high, and all the bold elements that help build true resilience. When I'm outside, it's nearly impossible to be sedentary—and movement matters. How could I write an entire book about raising resilient kids without talking about the importance of movement? The truth is that I didn't know how much movement mattered until I started moving.

What's wrong with society can be summed up in two facts. Obesity rates keep going up, and daily average step counts keep going down. We are getting fatter and less fit, year after year after year. You might be thinking this is great news for my business, but it isn't. The more comfortable we get as a society with being overweight and remaining still, the harder it is to rip people off the couch and get them out on the racecourse. Spartan is up for the challenge and we're committed to our mission, but if I had it my way, things would look a lot different.

Among the many benefits of exercise, a few deserve significant attention. You may have heard about the chemical benefits of exercise—the dopamine release, the adrenaline jolt, the endorphin hit—but there's another one that's a little less known but equally as important: endocannabinoids. Scientists call them the "don't worry, be happy" chemical, and they may be what's at play when athletes describe feeling a "runner's high." But here's the kicker: when these little suckers attach to receptors in the areas of the brain that regulate our response to stress—the amygdala (emotion center) and the prefrontal cortex—they help reduce stress, increase the availability of joy, and get you primed for social connection. Do you ever wonder why you want to connect with others after a run when you're normally an introvert? Endocannabinoids. Are you ever curious why an overwhelming day at work seems to fade away with an evening workout? Endocannabinoids.

Aside from these positive chemical changes, which are clear enough reasons to start moving your body, there is the huge psychological impact that exercise has on your self-esteem. Numerous studies have shown that regular exercise improves self-esteem, and here's why I think that matters. Remember those resilience data points (RDPs), the times in your life when you met a challenge head-on and pushed through? You can gather up mini-RDPs every time you work out and push yourself just a touch further than you did the day before. Think about it. How many times in the past have you wanted to quit during a workout, head back early when on a run, or cut short your bike ride but instead chose to keep going? If you can think of *at least* one time, you have an RDP for your capacity to push through something hard. We don't feel awesome after a workout just because of those feel-good chemicals. We feel awesome because we've done something awesome, and our confidence got a boost.

When people show up at my farm, overweight, out of shape, and ready to do things differently, I can see their self-esteem grow with each fitness gain. No matter the accomplishment—hiking up the mountain, stacking wood pellets, or doing morning stretches—their *I can't* begins to transform into an *I think I can*. The same thing happens at the Spartan starting line, where you can hear whispers of "I probably won't finish" and "There's no way I can do this!" At the finish line, the energy of those same people has completely shifted; their self-esteem is soaring. "That was awesome! I'll never say 'I can't' again!" they exclaim. Their physical feat combined with that discipline we discussed earlier creates this incredible cocktail of confidence.

Into the Wild:
For the Family

On Christmas Eve, most children are tucked into their beds, awaiting an indoor holiday that brings sugary treats and lots of stuff. We prefer to give our kids experiences rather than things. In 2017, when we were living in Japan, Courtney and I decided to fly into Sapporo, in the north, to take the family to a small resort town that we'd heard had insane skiing. It's near Nagano, where the 1998 Olympics were held. The kids were ten, eight, six, and three and were terrified that Santa wouldn't find them in such a remote place, but we assured them that his magic went everywhere.

After a long flight and a three-hour drive that got us in late, we walked into our hotel room and realized there had been some kind of mix-up. There were six of us and one tiny room with a mattress on the floor, a mini coffee table, and no additional furniture. We looked at one another and couldn't help but laugh. The guy at the hotel felt bad, so he took us out to a tiny apartment on a farm—more like a hut—and we broke through the snow and ice to get inside. That became our place for six or seven days. It was rustic, but beautiful. On Christmas Eve, Courtney went to a nearby gas station, the closest thing to a store, to see if she could find some Christmas presents. She bought what she thought were Pokémon cards. On Christmas morning, the kids opened their packs of cards, and brightly colored fruit roll-up things fell out. The kids howled with excitement, overjoyed that Santa had found them, knowing full well that Mom and Dad would never buy them that kind of candy. It's the little things, as Courtney likes to say.

Every day at 5 a.m. that week, a bird would fly into the room through a space beside the fan and wake us up with a song. Courtney felt like Cinderella. We would get up and go out to ski. It was like a dream: huge flakes falling on our eyelashes, bracing mountain air, the most insane powder ever. The trails were one challenge after another. My kids were in heaven being on the mountain all day, and they became much better skiers that week. It was the best Christmas break ever. Not a single screen was watched.

You don't have to take your kids on a trip or do anything fancy to have an outdoor adventure. You can play hockey with them in the street, hike the hill behind your house, challenge them to climb a rope in the backyard. Get your kids out of the house and active in all weather and all seasons. A happy, healthy life is dependent on a working body. There's no miracle powder, drink, food, or supplement that guarantees perfect health and extra time on earth. But there is a miracle available, and it's free. It's called VPA, or vigorous physical activity. And VPA will give your kids enormous advantages in life, including endurance; agility; strong bones and muscles; lean body composition; less anxiety; reduced risk of obesity; protection from type 2 diabetes, heart disease, and cancer; and greater optimism. If you don't instill in your children the habit and enjoyment of physical activity by age eight, you could deny them these incredible benefits.

Experts previously thought that physical activity started

to significantly decline during the teenage years, but a new study found that sedentary behavior may begin at a much younger age. The study, published in the journal *Pediatrics*, monitored six hundred European children ages six to eleven by having them wear an electronic armband that measured movement. Researchers found that kids moved a lot until around age eight. From there, they noticed a marked decline. Between ages six and eleven, the amount of moderate to vigorous physical activity declined by thirty minutes a day. At the same time, sedentary behavior increased by an average of 107 minutes per day.

How does this happen? The researchers didn't answer that question, but I'll make a guess. Kids are replacing running and other outside activity with sitting inside with their cell phones and video games. Why? Because parents aren't limiting screen time, and we aren't properly introducing the joy of physical play and exercise. Most kids will succumb to the addictive lure of video games rather than breaking a sweat climbing trees or playing stickball or riding a bike. It is up to parents to interest their children in physical activity at a young age. If you don't, the very clever folks who make apps and social media sites will find a way to entertain your kids instead. And they'll make a ton of money as your child becomes addicted to their products.

Outside playtime doesn't have to mean getting kids involved in organized sports or formal exercise programs, as great as they are. Any kind of vigorous play works: running, jumping, climbing, rolling, wrestling, swimming, building forts, chasing fireflies, skipping rocks. All types of physical activity strengthen their bodies and minds in diverse ways.

"Free play is so overlooked by parents," says Jeremy

Frisch, a former strength coach at Holy Cross University and owner of Achieve Performance Training in Clinton, Massachusetts, which focuses on fitness programs for younger kids. "Parents don't realize that kids need functional movement skills to get through life. Climbing trees, playing flashlight tag, pushing and pulling while wrestling on the grass, and learning how to fall—all those things develop proprioception skills and tactile feedback that they need to excel in sports later on."

Your kids can get all those benefits in just thirty to forty-five minutes a day, though I recommend up to two hours a day if you and yours can swing it. Get out there with them. They'll follow your lead and will love playing and laughing with you. Try these ideas to start:

- Find a hill. Sprint to the top and walk back down. Repeat. You can do this with stadium stairs at the local high school track, too. Race your kids. Kids love to compete!
- Got kids under five? Play an energetic version of Simon says or duck duck goose. Challenge them to a twenty-yard bear crawl or crab walk. Make it play, not work.
- Stretch your muscles while watching television with the kids. Whenever a commercial comes on, challenge them to a speed round of push-ups or burpees.
- Gather the whole family and play tag, kickball, red rover, buck buck, or hide-and-seek. Have wheelbarrow races. Think back to when you were a kid. What did you do on summer vacation? Every day

can have a little taste of summer vacation when you are outside with your kids.

Perhaps kids need nature even more than the rest of us. If you've ever built a sandcastle at the beach or a fort in the woods, you'll understand how the outdoors are a canvas for the imagination, for inventing what's possible. Kids' bodies and minds need many hours of outdoor play. This is how they will invent the future.

THE STRUGGLE WITH SCREENS

Screens are rapidly taking over the time that was once occupied by hopscotch, games of tag, and running around the park or woods. The sedentary activity of staring at a screen is sucking the life out of our kids by significantly reducing their time outdoors in the fresh air. And if you are allowing this to happen by turning away and binge-watching Netflix, you're contributing to the problem.

Billions of dollars go into making software and apps addictive and stimulating. Think about the way we adults scroll through social media platforms; it's a virtual slot machine giving our brains that dopamine hit that makes us feel good and want more. Kids can't regulate their time as adults do, and they don't have enough self-control to be discerning. If it were up to me, we wouldn't have screens at all. Screens aren't going to just disappear, though, so we've got to parent our children through this.

I'm no fan of video games, social media, or TV for one main reason. Our relationship with electronics is harming our youth, causing them to be woefully out of shape, disconnected from nature, unhealthy, and both physically and mentally weak. Studies show that today's children are less fit than their parents were as kids. We are failing our children, and we have to work together to change these scary trends and statistics:

- Only one in three children are physically active every day.
- About one in three children are either overweight or obese in the United States.
- On average, kids spend more than seven hours a day using TVs, computers, smartphones, and other electronic devices.
- In one study, children who exceeded the two hours of recommended daily screen time performed worse on a test that analyzed their memory, analytic, and language abilities.
- New diagnoses of type 2 diabetes among youth ages ten to nineteen are increasing at the alarming rate of 4.8 percent per year.

This last statistic is truly frightening. Having type 2 diabetes means that these kids may develop diabetes-related complications at such a young age that they are impacted for the rest of their lives. "This profoundly lessens their quality of life, shortens their life expectancy, and increases health care costs," says Dr. Guiseppina Imperatore, an epidemiologist with the National Center for Chronic Disease Prevention and Health Promotion.

HOW TO BUCK THE TREND

We have to lead by example. Parents who explore, enjoy adventure, and move their bodies often have kids who do the same. According to the American Council on Exercise, in families with physically active parents, kids are more than three times more likely to be active than kids whose parents are not active. By contrast, studies by the American Academy of Child and Adolescent Psychiatry show that when one parent in a family is obese, there's a 50 percent chance that their children will be obese; the presence of two obese parents raises the odds to 80 percent.

In addition to powering down and taking our kids out of the house and up hills, one technique that Courtney and I have found effective for curbing technology use is extracting precommitments through discussion. I got this idea from Nir Eyal's great book *Indistractable: How to Control Your Attention and Choose Your Life*. We've explained to our kids that gaming and social media get in the way of doing other meaningful things. To get access to the gaming systems or TV, our children must complete their chores, their reading, their schoolwork, their Mandarin, their workouts—whatever it is they have committed to accomplishing in life. Here's rule 2—Earned, Not Given—in action. Playing games, scrolling on their phones, heck, just having a damn phone—those are not birthrights. They've got to earn the time that they spend on those things. Dr. L notes that year after year parents feel more powerless to control their children's use of screens. "I will often hear parents say, 'Well, I can't just take their phone away.' Actually, that's exactly what you can do," she says. "Parents are so afraid of the tantrum and attitude that will follow the removal that they succumb to the idea that they don't have any power. Parents need to parent-up and do what's right for their kid, not what's easy and avoidant."

Finally, nobody in my house gets a major technology purchase without accomplishing something incredible. Catherine had to achieve academic and fitness goals to get a cell phone. I challenged Charlie to climb a rope to earn an Xbox, and the kid made his hands bloody climbing the rope day after day. You have to admire his tenacity. Now he says it wasn't worth it because he so rarely gets to play it, but I'll bet when he's older he'll remember those rope climbs more fondly than any video game.

The most important thing is to prioritize movement over screen time. Children are designed to move every single day of their lives. Kids need exercise for proper physical development and behavior. They should want to move naturally on their own, but, hey, they're kids. Sometimes you've got to nudge them, and if nudging doesn't work, then you've got to push. If they've been kidnapped by the electronic screen monsters, you have to get involved. It is your responsibility as a parent to intervene. If you find you need a crowbar to pry your kid's hands from the video game controller, then by all means grab a crowbar (or better, a kettlebell). You might have heard that a body at rest stays at rest unless acted on by a force. Well, you can be that force.

KIDS GOTTA MOVE!

We can all agree that school is important. Studying helps the brain develop, and learning a second language gives kids a competitive edge. But none of that matters if the vessel that stores all of this amazing information isn't healthy. Many parents are prioritizing mental intelligence and book smarts over physical activity. Kids come home from a long day at school and head straight to their room to get their homework done. Or parents keep their youngest ones inside because the weather is less than ideal, planting them in front of the TV.

Physical activity is essential. And I'm not talking about exercise for the goal of achieving a particular body type. I'm talking about respecting your body and teaching your kids to respect theirs as well. Physical activity of some kind, any kind, is essential for healthy brain development, muscle memory, and building confidence.

Your children have energy and need physical expression and activity to release and manage that energy. Encourage your children to be active and move their bodies. Teach your kids early on that the body is an important vessel that deserves respect and attention. Teach them that movement is an amazing way to engage in this process of life. And get out there with them. Throw the football around, grab the jump rope, climb a tree, or go for a walk in the woods. Whatever activity you choose, get moving!

As you begin to prioritize movement and exercise as a family, you'll witness the benefits pretty quickly. You'll see the difference in the behavior and attitudes of your children, especially the teenagers. You'll find that exercise makes your kids calm in body and spirit. On days when they don't get exercise, you'll know it. They'll be groggy, mopey, moody. They won't eat or sleep well. I'm convinced that if more kids exercised first thing in the morning before going to school, it would be easier for them to focus in class, and there'd be a lot fewer kids on ADHD medications.

SPARK FREE PLAY IN NATURE

We live in an over-productive, hyperstimulated society. And this lifestyle is being passed down to our children through overscheduling, excessive screen time, and nonstop structured activities. As a result, they are missing out on an essential brain-building exercise that stimulates creativity, fuels their imagination, and allows them to exert their bodies and minds freely and wildly. That exercise is free play.

For some of the reasons we've explored thus far—fear of judgment, increased risk, and aversion to failure—many parents have signed up for the additional job of micromanaging their kids. They over-supervise to ensure safety; they over-schedule to ensure their children are busy; and they over-manage to ensure that their child is highly productive. The problem with this approach is that parents are overlooking the amazing benefits of free play. They deprive their children of the opportunity to run around in the backyard without structured games or to simply return home from school without a prescheduled activity waiting for them.

Free play not only helps kids develop their creative resources and enhance their imagination but also aids in the fine-tuning of decision-making and problem-solving skills. Think about it: whether it's your thirteen-year-old who is bored on a Saturday or your five-year-old who isn't sure which toy to play with, both have to figure out a way to occupy their time, maintain their attention, and learn from whatever they have at hand. It's an awesome exercise in learning how to be self-sufficient.

Give your kids more freedom, especially in nature. Put them outside and give them an opportunity to figure out for themselves how they want to play or relax. Take away just one scheduled activity and see how they manage with a little free time. Sit back and take a break from micromanaging.

Structured fitness routines are great, but it's also really important for kids to have time for play in a completely unstructured way. And it's equally important that they play outside instead of inside. According to a recent survey of twelve thousand parents in ten countries, one-third of children aged five to twelve spend less than thirty minutes outside each day. By contrast, US prisoners are guaranteed two hours a day of outdoor time by law. In other words, criminals at a maximum-security prison are getting more time outdoors each day than your kids.

No wonder childhood obesity and type 2 diabetes have become significant health problems for adolescents. Kids just aren't meeting the recommendations for daily physical activity. But the effects go beyond physical health. Numerous studies suggest that lack of adequate outdoor play is associated with poor performance in school. In fact, a recent study from Norway found that children ages four through seven who spent more time outside during child-care showed fewer inattention-hyperactivity symptoms. They also performed better on tests of the executive mental functions that enable us to filter distractions, plan, and prioritize.

Match your kids' interests with movement. "Parents need to find opportunities where fitness is the outcome, not the goal," says David Jack, a fitness trainer and adviser for the International Youth Conditioning Association. Do this by observing what brings joy for your kids, and try to find ways to build physical movement into those interests. One parent noticed that his son spent an enormous amount of time looking at aircraft online and building paper airplanes. He suggested that they build paper and balsa wood airplanes together and launch them from the top of the stadium at a local high school football field. They spent a fun hour running up and down the stairs to launch and retrieve the airplanes and got a great leg and cardio workout. What a brilliant way to incorporate fitness into an otherwise sedentary activity!

A NOTE ON BOREDOM

I don't enjoy being bored. I prefer to be on the move—whether literally moving my body or moving my mind. Sitting still is hard for me. But we are too quick to alleviate boredom—both as adults and as parents. When my kids walk aimlessly around the house, it drives me crazy. "I'm bored" is an invitation to join me in a hike up the mountain with a log, to jog several times around the block backward, or to sort our nail drawer—so my kids typically know better. My father was exactly the same way. If I complained about being bored, he would find me the most mundane, menial task to do, and it felt like pure torture. It was a lesson in complaining.

I have noticed, however, that our society has a problem with boredom. We can't tolerate it. Dr. L has an interesting take on boredom, and it starts with our belief system. "We have become a society that not only idealizes the non-stop hustle but also sees productivity as a status symbol," she says. "The busier we are, the more important we seem. This is bleeding into how we see our kids as well. If they're bored, we feel compelled to find something for them to do and keep them productive. The truth is, this is crushing our youth and killing their attention spans. If you want your kids to stop complaining when they have to wait in the car or quit whining while they're waiting at a restaurant for their food to be delivered, then you have to teach them the art of being bored, of dealing with *not having something to do*. It seems like a silly skill, but think about when you were a kid and you didn't have all of today's technology and streaming devices to keep you stimulated. You probably did crossword puzzles, played I-spy at the restaurant, or just stared out the window in the car. And it served you well because you can tolerate boredom now. You don't have be stimulated and entertained every single second of the day. Give your kid the same gift by letting them be bored every once in a while."

Are Your Kids Afraid of Mosquitos?

A 2011 survey by the Nature Conservancy found that 80 percent of children claimed their unwillingness to go outside was due to "discomfort" caused by external factors such as bugs and heat. Just under half (49 percent) said they just weren't interested in spending time in nature. Is this really okay with us as parents? Are we so afraid that our children will see a bug that we are willing to put their future health and happiness at risk?

Exercise Makes Kids Smarter

Tell your kid to take a break from that textbook, go outside, and run around. Many studies have shown that getting exercise outdoors improves kids' brain function:

- Researchers from the University of North Texas found that kids who get regular aerobic activity score higher on reading and math tests.
- University of Illinois scientists measured the brain size of a group of nine- and ten-year-olds using magnetic resonance imaging equipment and found that kids who were physically active had larger hippocampi than kids who were sedentary. The active kids also scored higher on memory tests. The hippocampus is the part of the brain associated with long-term memory, but it also regulates emotions and plays a role in spatial navigation.
- A study in the journal *Pediatrics* determined that children who ran around playing soccer, tag, and other outdoor games for at least seventy minutes a day showed greater improvement in thinking and multitasking skills compared to children who weren't as active.

Exercise Lengthens Attention Span
Rod Dixon

Rod Dixon is a four-time Olympian runner who won a bronze medal in the 1,500-meter race at the 1972 Olympic Games. He founded Kidsmarathon, an organization that encourages kids to love running.

When I was in school, my teachers would write "fidgets," "lacks concentration," "looks out the window," and "disturbs others" all over my reports. Today, I would be medicated, but back then one of my teachers realized that all I needed was some exercise. He would send me out of class for something and I would run around while I did it and then I would be able to focus when I got back. Exercise recalibrated me. Now, when I'm talking to a classroom full of kids about Kidsmarathon, I see them squirming if I try to talk for twenty minutes straight. So, I get them up every five minutes to do some exercise, and then I've got their attention for another five minutes.

Help Your "Shy" Child Grow
Dr. Lara Pence

A lot of parents come to me for advice on getting their "shy" child out of his or her shell. For starters, let's get one thing clear—being "shy" or introverted is not a sign of weakness. In fact, it can be a real sign of strength. (If you have a "shy" child, I recommend you read *Quiet Power: The Secret Strengths of Introverted Kids*, a spin-off of Susan Cain's amazing bestseller, *Quiet*.)

I always encourage parents to remember that we each get our energy from different sources. Just because your kiddo may prefer reading alone on the park bench to playing on the monkey bars with others doesn't mean that they won't adjust well in life or that they need to be confined to indoor activities. Some of the most brilliant and well-adjusted individuals are introverts. Try to meet your children where they are. Encourage social interaction, yes, but also let them be who they are. Here are some other techniques you could try to help your introvert grow.

Schedule one-on-one time with other kids. This may be more effective than large play groups or social gatherings. The more kids at an event, the more overwhelming it may be for your child, so keep it small, starting with just one other kiddo.

Don't try to manufacture a best friend. Making friends is hard. It takes time. There is so much pressure for kids to have a "best friend" at every age. Sometimes kids may go through a season not having that one special person. Be patient. Tolerate your own distress and desire to save them. Remind them that it will happen in time. Avoid trying to figure out how to get them a friend. Let them navigate it on their own, but be there to encourage them along the way and celebrate the occasion when it does happen.

Use your child's interests to facilitate group interaction. Not a playgroup where you stick around, but maybe a camp, an after-school activity, or a team sport that aligns with something they've expressed an interest in. Using the interest itself as the stepping stone to more exposure to peers and friendships is best because they inherently have something to talk about or something in common. If they come home, tell you they hate it, and want to quit, don't be discouraged—and *don't* pull them out of it until it's run its scheduled course. Again, let them navigate it, figure out their own feelings, explore this new world. Your child may never prefer a group activity over solitary time, but giving them the opportunity is important.

In Conclusion

I'll say it again . . . fit parents who demonstrate a love for the outdoors will inspire fit and active kids who also love the outdoors. But even if you are afraid of mosquitos and getting dirty, you can find creative and fun ways to get your kids moving. Your enthusiasm and love will help them see the fun in flying a kite, chasing lightning bugs, or sprinting to the mailbox. Use your ingenuity; you don't have to be a wilderness survival expert like Bear Grylls to get your kids outside and moving. You just have to care enough about their health to make playtime fun and to move it outdoors for a bit of fresh air every day.

A healthy relationship with your body is all about seeing it as an extremely important vessel that allows you to make your mark on the world. You can't make your mark if you can't leave your house because you're too overweight. You can't make your mark if you're attached to hospital tubes and IVs because you've had five heart attacks in five years. And you can't make your mark *as a parent* if you're not on this planet. You've got to value your body and the amazing things it can do—and teach your kids this same lesson.

Raw Courage

Getting a Grip on Fear

> The most difficult thing is the decision to act, the rest is merely tenacity.
>
> —Amelia Earhart

In 2000, I went to a race in Nantucket, Massachusetts, that I wasn't even signed up to do. It was a short, relay-style race with multiple disciplines. I showed up with a bunch of buddies, and we figured, *Why the hell not? We're all relatively fit; we'll crush it.* We decided that I would do the beach run with the heavy backpack. Medium distance, extra weight for a bulky challenge—my cup of tea.

I completed my section and tagged my teammate, who was slated to swim across the bay, a welcome handoff considering that if there's one thing that scares me, it's sharks. When I was ten years old, my father let me watch *Jaws*. Holy fuck. I was terrified. I avoided the ocean whenever I could, and even showers became precarious. I would spread my feet as far from the drain as possible just in case the shark decided to make a star appearance up the pipes. It was illogical, I realize now, but back then I was certain that I was in danger.

So needless to say, when I tapped my teammate's hand and he bounded into the water, I felt relieved that I wasn't the one going in. But here's the thing about me: when my brain—or anyone else, for that matter—tells me, *Don't do it*, I feel an immediate desire to do the opposite. It's one reason I'm so competitive, but it's also what's made me successful in business. So when my friend dove into the water and my brain said, *Joe, don't go in—you don't have to, and there may be sharks*, I thought, *Well, here goes. I've got to do it now.* And into the ocean I went.

Was I scared? Fuck yeah! Nantucket is known for shark sightings, and my childhood fear had not been eradicated in any way, shape, or form. But that fear gremlin in my head activated the challenge signal, and I took the bait. I ditched my shoes, swam across the bay, slugged up to the shore, legs all wobbly, and started running to the last leg of the race—why not? I'd completed two sections of the relay; I might as well just bang the whole thing out. And that's when my life made a beeline for awesome because standing at the edge of the sand with a crowd of spectators was my future wife. The universe sent me the best reward on the planet for facing a huge fear, and the rest is history.

Fear is everywhere and in each and every one of us. It doesn't discriminate, and it's not going anywhere. You can choose to let fear stand in your way, or you can learn to act anyway. I'm an "act anyway" kind of guy. When I feel fear, it often feels like a signal for me to do what is necessary. I know the brain science—most of the time, the discomfort that arises from fear is just my lizard brain stepping in because it interprets something as a threat. But I've realized that what's on the other side of fear is often fantastic. Case in point: my wife. I would never have met Courtney if I didn't take that plunge into the ocean and face my fear. I didn't stand there evaluating the situation, performing some kind of cost-benefit analysis. I just *went*.

I meet people who have done some of the most extraordinary things, and not one of them says, *I've never been afraid*. In fact, most of them say that they've met their most courageous self when they were afraid to do something but chose to do it anyway. Courtney and I tell our kids all the time that it's not about getting rid of the fear; it's about acting anyway. The problem is that fear can be a visceral experience. We get bogged down by the physical sensations—the racing heart, the sweaty palms, the shaky legs—and so we retreat and say no thanks. Every time we do this, we reinforce the idea that our fear was worth avoiding, when more than likely it wasn't. Let's unpack this a bit and take a look at the neuroscience. I'm a huge believer that when you know what your brain is doing, you can start to make different choices.

Respect Fear as Natural

Fear is a good thing. It has helped our species survive for millions of years. It comes in lots of varieties and intensities: fear of heights, fear of snakes, fear of public speaking, fear of failure, fear of losing a loved one, fear of rejection, fear of criticism or embarrassment, and even fear of success. Whatever form it takes, fear triggers the primitive physiological response of fight, flight, or freeze.

Our primal fear response originates in what's known as the "reptilian brain," the oldest part of our brain, the amygdala. The work of pioneering neuroscientist Joseph LeDoux of New York University revealed why this part of our brain is so powerful: the amygdala acts before the rest of our intellect has time to think. LeDoux's research shows that the initial sight or sound of a potential threat travels immediately from the eyes or ears to the thalamus, and then directly to the amygdala. A second brain signal emerges from the thalamus and is routed to the neocortex, the thinking brain, which ruminates on this data before forming a conclusion—*Run! Stand still! Fight like hell!*

The reality that, in times of danger, our neural pathways bypass the thinking brain and take a shortcut to the primitive brain is incredibly useful. It saves our butt when we hear the screech of brakes and jump out of the way of a car in the nick of time. But there is a downside: your reptilian brain can become activated by benign or perceived threats, as well as genuine ones. Whenever we start something new or take steps toward our dream goals, the lizard brain starts telling us to slow down, be careful, and be fearful. Rather than letting us move out of our comfort zone, the amygdala takes command and forces us to procrastinate, make excuses, and doubt our abilities. This happens throughout our lives if we don't learn true resilience. Interviewing for a job or giving a presentation may not be a life-threatening event, but your amygdala may react as if it were. When the amygdala is triggered to take control of our organism, it creates a fear cocktail; our heartbeat surges, we start sweating, our eyes widen, and our muscles tense as we prepare to fight or flee, or everything shuts down and we freeze in the shadow of danger.

However, this fight, flight, or freeze response is also a powerful tool for action. Fear is a high-octane fuel that can power action and our future success, if we look at it that way. Once you learn how to accept and quiet your lizard brain, you can accept uncertainty and even embrace it.

Respect Fear as Normal

Everybody feels fear. It's the response to fear that varies from person to person. How do we become a person with true resilience who uses fear as high-octane fuel rather than experiencing it as a paralyzing tonic? Here's your answer: get moving.

The worst thing fear can do to you is get in your way and keep you stagnant. Sure, it's a body signal you should take note of. But when you stand still and let irrational thinking take up more and more space, you slowly retreat. My solution is to just get moving. When fear pops up, I notice quickly and then step on the gas pedal before fear nails my feet to the floor.

Dr. L recommends giving your emotion a name, a strategy that helps her clients deal with fear. "This is a tactic that you can use with any emotion," she says. "And it's easy to do. Just name the fear. Literally. Sometimes you can think of a past person who has invoked that emotion and use that same name or just pick any name you like. For example, if a bully at school named Henry scared you as a kid, whenever you recognize that fear is showing up, you say to yourself, *Oh, Henry is here to veer me off course.* It may sound silly, but it works. High-performance athletes have used this tactic when self-doubt starts to creep in. They give it a name and tell Sally, Bob, Tim, or Candice to fuck off. Using this strategy allows you to detach from overidentifying with the emotion itself. So instead of feeling like a *fearful person*, you are just a person who is *feeling fear*."

Elizabeth Gilbert, bestselling author of *Eat Pray Love*, does something similar when she's writing a new book. Sometimes, when she starts to get some ideas and put words down on the page, fear suddenly appears, causing her to experience panic and shame and doubt. *Is this idea even good? What if this character is a stupid cliché? What if I'm in over my head with this plot?* Fear takes over and she can't write anything. Gilbert redirects this fear by imagining it as a person. She allows fear on the journey of writing a book, and even welcomes it, but she doesn't let fear drive the car . . . under any circumstance. Fear is always present, but never in control.

This is precisely how I use fear in my life. I consider it a welcome guest at all times, but if it tries to get smart with me and take over, I take notice and then just get moving and put it in its place. Fear isn't going to stop me, but its presence shouldn't be denied.

Getting a Grip on Fear

I realize that I may be a bit of an anomaly. Not everyone who is afraid of sharks is going to be able to just say, "Fuck it," and plunge into the ocean. Let's break down what I'm really doing in steps so that you can see that what I do is completely possible for you, too.

1   **Notice and name fear.** Here's where you need to tune in. If you're not paying attention, fear can overcome your entire body and wreak havoc on your mind. Understanding how fear shows up in your body is an incredible tool. As soon as you start to hear that fear gremlin tell you no, or when you feel your heart racing or other physical responses, you can call it fear. Don't be afraid to call it what it is. I sometimes encounter people who tell me they're not afraid of anything, and it's total bullshit. We are all afraid of something. Even if what you're afraid of is not becoming your most resilient self—well, that's still fear.

2   **Shift from threat to opportunity.** As discussed above, the feeling of fear is coming from your brain's interpretation of something as a threat. But just because your brain tells you so doesn't mean you have to listen. Fear can provide incredible opportunities. Fear can help you build confidence when you face a fear. Fear can help you practice when you aren't sure if you're prepared enough. Fear can remind you of who matters in your life when you imagine their absence. And fear can make you a better parent by forcing you to pay more attention. When fear

comes up, quickly consider the opportunity that's being presented. Don't get stuck in a long-drawn-out analysis, but do try to move from your lizard brain to your thinking one.

3 **Move.** In the previous chapter I talked about the benefits of exercise, including how it calms your stress response. Let that work in your favor. When you're fearing the presentation you have to give in thirty minutes, go up and down the fire escape stairs a few times. When you're scared to get on the plane, walk the jetway instead of sitting in the boarding area. When you're feeling fear about your kid's violin performance, bike to the concert hall instead of driving there. Fight your brain's first impulse with a dose of its own medicine. Move around and get those chemicals working in your favor.

4 **Make a choice.** This is where there is no hack, no trick, no tip I can give that will get you out of making that choice. You just have to make it. Do you want to get in the ocean like a badass, or do you want to remain on the sand, a timid ten-year-old boy who shudders at the thought of going in? At some point you've got to take the plunge. Like many things in this book, you don't build the skill unless you take action. This is where *doing the hard stuff* comes in. Your hard stuff might look different than mine. Perhaps sharks are no problem for you, but you wouldn't step foot in the reptile section of the zoo. You won't get used to snakes if you never expose yourself to them. You may wonder, *But if I live my whole life afraid of snakes, what does it matter?* Well, you never know what life may throw at you, so you need to be ready for anything.

No matter what scares you, remember that fear is just a feeling. Dr. L says, "So many people are confusing fact with feeling. The fear signal is immediately being attended to as if it were the behavior guru, an expert worth listening to at all times. *Fear is telling me not to, so I shouldn't.* Fear is just a feeling. And honestly, it's an awesome one. The physiological response of fear and excitement are so similar, practically identical in fact. If we can remember this, we can learn to build up a greater tolerance to fear and engage in our lives more courageously."

Decision-Making Fear

Many people are afraid in every part of life. Of course, fear shows up all the time, not just when we're out on a dangerous hike or getting married or buying a house. We make many tiny decisions every day, and those decisions have big consequences.

The tool I like to use for fear-response training is the acronym *BRAIN.* When faced with a decision, ask yourself these questions:

> What are the BENEFITS of doing this?
> What are the RISKS of doing this?
> What are the ALTERNATIVES, and what are the benefits
>   and risks of each?
> What is my INSTINCT?
> What if I do NOTHING?

I adhere to this practice for decision-making in every part of my life. I find that thinking through a problem, big or small, takes fear out of the equation.

Sometimes fear isn't rational, and it ends up in our bodies before we know it. In those moments, fear has already moved from your brain to your physical being, and the effects are taking hold. In my house, we use the *BRAIN* acronym in another way (created by Dr. L) to help the entire family move through anxiety and fear when it shows up in the body. Use this easy-to-remember acronym whenever a fear response starts to bubble up:

BREATHE. Take some deep breaths.

RECOGNIZE. Name what you are feeling (fear, worry, embarrassment, nervousness, etc.).

ARMOR. Identify the tools you need to be brave in this situation. For adults, this could be a breathing exercise, a phone call to a trusted mentor, or a reminder of previous RDPs. For kids, this could be a favorite stuffed animal.

IMAGINE a win. Think about how you will feel after you have faced your fear.

NEXT. Take the next best step. Move forward.

Raw Courage:
For the Family

As you've learned from some of my stories, my kids have shown me time and again how overcoming fear has nothing to do with getting rid of it. They have reminded me that true courage is not the absence of fear but rather the strength to tackle it head-on. When it comes to kids, one of the best lessons I've learned is that fear can be fun.

When Catherine was just five years old, we were living in Vermont and all the kids were participating in ski racing at Pico Mountain. The older kids loved taking part in the Mountain Dew Challenge every spring. The kids would register in the morning, receive their race bib, and then head up the mountain. What made it special was that an announcer introduced each kid over the loudspeaker, which was always a hit with them.

One year, I took Jack and Charlie up the mountain to race while Courtney hung back with Catherine, who was not old enough to race at that time. While I stood in line beside the boys, waiting for the race to start, I suddenly noticed this tiny little child jet off the chairlift and cruise quickly in front of Jack, who was next up. I peered carefully through my goggles and realized that this little pink nugget who just cut in front of Jack was Catherine!

She jumped into the course path and barreled down the

mountain with my wife skiing after her. I heard, "Catherine! Wait!" coming from Courtney, but our courageous girl was off and running. There was no stopping her. It was a riot to see this puffy pink bubble cruising down Pico Mountain with the announcer shouting joyfully, "And it looks like we have a bandit on the course!"

When Jack, Charlie, and I got down the mountain, Courtney could not stop laughing. Catherine had no idea that she had done anything wrong and was so pleased with herself for doing what all the big kids were doing. Both Courtney and I were beaming with pride. Catherine showed raw courage in that moment, and it is still one of our favorite family memories.

My entire life is based on running headfirst into a challenge and pushing the roadblocks out of my way. Obstacle racing is purposeful suffering, and I've been practicing it for years. Behavioral scientists and therapists use a similar practice to help clients manage stress and anxiety; it's called "stress inoculation training" (SIT). Simply put, you can develop the skills to manage stressful situations by repeatedly exposing yourself to the things that you fear or that create anxiety. What we do at Spartan, and what I've done my whole life, is not the classic practice of SIT, but it's darn close—and we all need a whole lot more of it.

When it comes to my kids, I'm not cavalier about throwing them into stressful situations, but I'm not afraid to do so. As parents, our number one job is to set our children up for success, so it's tempting to shield them from adversity. I've learned, however, that this is a mistake, and there's no reason to protect our children from tough stuff because kids are a lot more courageous than we think. Dr. L notes that we parents often project our own fears onto our children. For example, we might arrive at our kids' climbing competition, take one look at the route up to the top, feel sheer terror, and tell them, "Wow, it's okay for you to be scared," before we even determine whether they're afraid!

My wife and I move our family to different countries every couple of years when particular business opportunities pop up. I'll jump on these opportunities, while other parents tell me, "We can't move our family until they're out of the house. It would be too hard on them." I've been surprised to find that with every move, our children have adjusted more quickly than we have. They no longer fear new environments or strange languages. They embrace new cultures and are curious about new traditions. They make new friends with the snap of a finger. The pandemic and subsequent impacts have led many families to consider moving. If you can do it, do it! Dr. L moved her family just a few years ago. She and her husband wanted to be closer to the mountains, so from Dallas to Colorado they went. She prioritized her values—family and adventure—and it's served her family well. Her oldest child, Parker, got into climbing. Her youngest, Keaton, got into farming, and they're in heaven!

If you believe a move would benefit your family, try to find a way to make it work. Move to a healthier city or a smaller town. Wake up in a place that's more in alignment with who you and your family are. Pushing our whole family out of our comfort zone hasn't destroyed us. Quite the opposite. It has shown us how to unlock some of the potential within ourselves.

There's a Spartan whose courage inspires me, and he's twelve years old. Before the COVID-19 pandemic slowed things down, Samuel "Shades" Koehler was running obstacle course races (OCRs) every month. He's a regular on the podium at Spartan Kids races in the southern United States, and he's won multiple first, second, and third place prizes. His achievements are impressive on their own, but they take on a whole new meaning when you learn that Samuel is visually impaired. He has achromatopsia, a rare eye condition that affects an estimated one in thirty thousand people worldwide and is characterized by a partial or total absence of color vision. It seriously limits Samuel's ability to see in bright light, so he wears dark glasses to improve his daytime vision. His disability has locked him out of sports like baseball, football, soccer, and hockey—he has trouble tracking a ball or puck when it's headed toward him—but he asked his parents if he could try an OCR when he saw a commercial for Spartan on TV.

Imagine making your way through the two-plus miles of a Spartan Kids obstacle course race, crawling under ropes in the mud, climbing up the A-frame, pushing through tree branches, hopping through a sea of tires. Now imagine doing all that and more with impaired vision.

Samuel decided to start Spartan with a noncompetitive race, and his older sister Rachael served as his guide through that first course. He says, "The race directors were aware of my vision issue and allowed me to walk through the course, just like they did, on the night before. I used this to try and remember where the obstacles were and get an idea of the course." He fell down several times during the open race, but he got back up and came in fourth. Then he went on to a competitive race. He says, "I was definitely afraid at my first competitive Spartan race because it was the first time I was running by myself. I overcame my fear by praying before the race and remembering how many people were there supporting me." He came in first.

"It was very nerve-racking for my husband and me," Samuel's mom, Debbie Koehler, remembers. "We knew he would fall. He would run into trees. He might even wander off course because he can't see the orange tape that lines the course. But as parents we don't want to hold him back, so we just thought, *Why not?*" Sam went on to dominate Spartan Kids races, and now he's training for more.

Samuel sometimes gets scratched and bruised as he competes, but he's developed a method of shielding his face with his arm or elbow, and he keeps going. I've no doubt we are witnessing the emergence of a champion as we watch Shades thrive on the Spartan courses. What is it that gives this kid the courage to face intimidating and frightening things? What gives him the guts to keep going and *win* after he falls off an obstacle or gets scratched by something he can't see? Samuel admits he was scared when he first started Spartan, yet he never got paralyzed by his fear. He was able to work through that feeling, perhaps even using it to push himself forward. Why? I'd venture to guess it's not only because he's had lifelong experience with adversity, but also because of the way he has been led by his parents. They were nervous for Samuel, but they didn't let their protective instinct keep him from challenging himself.

HELPING YOUR KIDS BUILD COURAGE

What happens if your kids are not exhibiting anything near Samuel's level of courage and mettle? What do we do when we suspect our children's timidity and fear are holding them back? Think back to Debbie Koehler's emotional response as she watched her visually impaired son take part in a race in which he would likely fall down, run into things, and maybe even fail. The experience was "nerve-racking," she says, but she didn't let the emotion get the best of her, for Samuel's sake. One of the critical first steps in helping your kids manage their fear response is to become an expert at managing your own. Kids pick up on the energy of their parents so, as we've discussed before, it's imperative that you model good fear control. Practice the four-step process outlined earlier in this chapter whenever you can so that you learn to tolerate your own fearful or anxious feelings. You don't have to hide this from your kids. Your children will never know what courage is if they don't see you afraid but doing something anyway. If planes make you freak out and you've got a big trip coming up, let your kids know that you're a little afraid but you're going to use your strategies to help manage the fear and hop on that plane regardless. As you become more of an expert at managing your own fears, your kids will try to do the same with theirs!

HELP, BUT DON'T FIX OR MINIMIZE

One of the most common phrases that you'll hear parents say to their child is, "Don't be scared." We say it all the time— before a test or competition, on the high board at the pool, when the power goes out. It just pops out of our mouth uncontrollably. But guess what? It doesn't help. As we've learned in this chapter, fears can be totally irrational. Was a shark really going to find its way through the plumbing and attack me in the shower? No. But logic didn't matter, and the advice "Don't be scared" would not have been helpful. A better response would be, "Well, that's okay. You can be scared and still do _____ [whatever that might be]." Remember, we want to teach our kids to persevere in the face of fear—not try to get rid of it and certainly not to avoid it.

Parents are also too quick to respond to a child's fear and jump in to "make it better." Allow your kids to experience distress and learn to tolerate it. Teach them to manage fears and turn them from threat to opportunity. See if they can come up with a way through their fear rather than doing it for them. This helps build confidence and lets them know that you believe in them!

Here are some other ways to help your kids start turning fear into fuel for positive action.

Define "Scary"—If You Can Name It, You Can Tame It

Teach your kids what fear is: it's just a feeling. And all feelings are just emotions, not facts that are set in stone. Research from the Yale Center for Emotional Intelligence has found that when we simply put a name on an emotion or fear, the intense emotional response in the brain is soothed and tamed. As Dr. Dan Siegel says, "If you can name it, you can tame it!" Remember what Dr. L talked about earlier? This tactic can be especially useful with younger kids because coming up with a silly name can really help to detach any fear immediately. It's not scary if you call it Boogers.

Befriend Intensity

Even intense feelings like, say, being afraid of the ocean can change. While you cannot teach your kids how to eliminate fear (remember, it's hardwired), you can help them control how they respond to it. Tell your children that feelings are not an accurate measure of what they can actually handle. Just because you are *more* afraid of something does not mean that you are *less* capable. In fact, sometimes we get *really* afraid of certain things because they matter so much to us. For example, if you have a high schooler who is really scared of taking his college entrance exams, well, that makes sense. He may be terrified that he won't get into his school of choice. Help your children uncover what matters to them and what their fear is attached to.

Also, remind them that fear and excitement can feel very similar. The physiological response to each is nearly identical, and this can work in your kids' favor. While your daughter may express fear about her big piano recital, she may also just be excited to finally showcase her talent. Help your kids shift their language from "I'm scared" to "I'm excited!"

Try Fear-Setting

Author and entrepreneur Tim Ferriss uses an amazing exercise he calls "fear-setting" whenever he feels anxious about something. You might try this quick activity with your kids. Have them answer three simple questions:

1. *What could go wrong?* Define the problem.
2. *How can I prevent that problem from happening?* Figure out actions you can take to overcome the problem.
3. *If it ends up going wrong anyway, how can I fix the problem?*

When your child comes up with the answers to those three questions, he or she begins to wrestle back some control and lessen the fear. The trick to overcoming fear is regaining a sense of being in control.

Help Kids Avoid Avoidance

One of the best things you can do for your kids—especially for teens who tend to be incredibly self-conscious—is to show them that avoidance of anxiety-producing situations is self-sabotage. The problem with giving in to our natural tendency to avoid the new and the scary is that habituation (growth) never happens. Every time we avoid what we are afraid of, we allow anxiety to win, and we fail to habituate ourselves to what scares us. In fact, when we avoid something, the fear grows stronger. We get the feel-good reward of avoiding the fear itself, and our brain says, *See! Avoiding the fear was the better choice. Keep doing it, and I'm going to make the fear more intense so you listen!* Make sure that you don't let your kids avoid the fear-inducing experiences.

Show Kids That Courage Isn't About Being Fearless

Show your kids that courage doesn't mean that you are not afraid. Samuel Koehler was very afraid when he started Spartan, but he used those feelings as fuel. We need to teach our kids to overcome their fears by *doing*, not by *waiting* until they are no longer afraid. For example, if your child is afraid of entering a competition, don't wait until the fear is gone to sign them up. Sign them up anyway. Encourage them to move toward the fear, not away from it. Then, when they participate, they have a resilience data point that gives them information about the truth of their fear (was it really worth worrying about?) and about their capacity to handle the frightening situation. The data point will demonstrate that fear does not have to stop them and that they have the strength to overcome obstacles. They will begin to internalize the thought, *I can still do things even when I am afraid. Fear is just a feeling, and it doesn't have power over me.*

STOP OVERPARENTING

Many adults overparent because of their own fear of failure. They are terrified that they will screw up as parents and that their children won't be happy, won't do well in school, won't make the team, won't get into college, will live in the basement as an adult. . . . You get the picture.

Are you worried about any of those possible outcomes? It's normal to have these concerns. After all, you want your kids to become healthy, happy, productive citizens. But it's unhealthy—and unhelpful—to allow these common fears to get out of hand and grow into fear-based parenting.

Where does this fear come from? "Normally, fear of failure as a parent is driven by three elements," Dr. L says. "Your own difficult experiences as a child; the pressure for perfection; and your desire to ensure that your child avoids rejection. When you operate from fear, the danger is that your child can become the embodiment of your greatest worry. You end up projecting your own fears onto your children, which they then absorb and act out. They may ultimately operate from the same position of fear."

Here's how it works in real life: Remember that time you got picked on in grade school for wearing unfashionable clothing? The experience was humiliating and had such an impact on you that you now excessively worry that your own child may be picked on if she is not careful with her style. You may try to keep your worry in check, but it seeps out as you shop diligently to ensure she has the coolest clothes, personally adjust her clothing each day, and plan out her accessories. Over time, your child absorbs the unspoken message that if she's not dressing "properly," she won't be liked by others. So she, too, begins to operate from a position of fear, becoming equally obsessive about her wardrobe, wearing the latest trends, and working diligently to protect herself from social rejection. Bam. Your fear has become her fear.

Another source of fear may be your relationship with other local parents. Parents often fear the judgment of their friends, in-laws, teachers, coaches, and communities. There is constant pressure to keep up with what everyone else is doing. Dr. L hears this kind of thing all the time in her practice. It sounds something like this: "Our daughter's friend Sarah is on the traveling field hockey team. Her parents cart her all over the state to games. Our daughter only plays locally, and we have to work instead of going to her games. She is falling behind. And we are bad parents." Parents like this may begin to think, *If I'm the perfect parent, I won't be judged.* They may believe that if their child has it all, they won't be viewed as a failure.

Catch yourself when you allow your fears and insecurities to guide your parenting. Remember that when you give your children less, you give them a chance to rise to the occasion. When you acknowledge that the world is imperfect and that you have limitations, such as the inability to take them to field hockey every day because you work, you give your kids the opportunity to solve problems, adapt, and find other interests. You are a great and imperfect parent.

What Kids Can Teach You About Fear

Rather than trying to teach your kids how to be courageous, maybe you need to become the student. Here are four things children can teach us about being fearless.

1 *Be yourself and you'll never go wrong.* My kids aren't afraid to sing or dance in public—or order a stranger to drop and give them thirty burpees (I might have played a role in that one)—because they know what matters to them, and they like who they are! They know what they like, and they're not afraid to show it. The world rewards the ambitious—those who are willing to run through walls to get what they want—and it all starts with being the purest version of yourself possible.

2 *Tomorrow is a new day.* With every move to a new town, I see the same pattern. Day 1: the kids hang around the house, afraid to venture too far. Day 2: they're so busy playing outside with their new friends that they don't want to come home for dinner. As adults, we tend to dwell on our troubles. If we fumble a presentation at work, it feels like the end of the world. *Will my boss forgive me? What*

will my colleagues think of me? Who cares? Tomorrow's a new day. Wake up and kick some ass.

3 **Wear your scars with pride.** As adults, we try to smooth our wrinkles, comb over our bald spots, and pretend our jobs and lives are perfect. Kids don't do that. If you let them explore the world freely and don't teach them that the area outside the fence is dangerous, they'll embrace their scrapes, bumps, and bruises as bragging rights. Life is like a sports car. If you don't ding yourself here and there, you're probably taking the corners too slowly. Life's little fender benders lead to big learning.

4 **Curiosity opens doors.** I'm endlessly fascinated by new people and things. That's why I accept every networking meeting I can—and perhaps that explains why I'm constantly open to trying new things at Spartan. I see that same inquisitiveness in my kids, and nothing makes me happier. Why? Because curiosity is the key to success in business and in life. It constantly leads you down new paths and positions you in front of new doors. You never know what awaits you, and that's what makes this journey so exciting. Yes, you'll have doubts. But for best results, make like a child and be brave.

Courage can be learned. Bravery can be developed. Fearlessness can be trained. Your children will need all of these traits at some point in their lives. Whether facing down a bully, stepping onto the high diving board, sitting for a college entrance exam, asking for a raise, or tackling an important social issue, your children's attitude will determine their success. Embrace and work with fear early on; pretty soon, your little ones will be the breakout star of their own life, unflappable, unbreakable, and unmistakably fearless.

The Courage to Allow Your Kids to Fly

It was a dreary day at Citi Field in New York City. Heidi Krupp-Lisiten, a PR consultant who helped out with Spartan, was on the sidelines of a Spartan Sprint with her son, eight-year-old Caden Lisiten. The plan was for her husband, Darren, to run with me, and for Caden to run with a group of friends his age. Heidi expected Darren to keep an eye on the boy throughout the race. She remembers, "We're near the first obstacle, the wall, and Joe comes over and says, 'Listen, you helicopter! Step aside. He's mine. I got this." Then he grabs my son and takes him over the wall with him." Heidi knew and trusted me, but she says, "I felt totally panicked. My little guy was racing with Joe De Sena. It was his first race." Caden took off with me, and when he found his rhythm in the race, I let him go on his own. Says Heidi, "There was a moment in the race when Caden picked up the thirty-pound sandbag and fell backward. Then he got up, tried again, and did it. This was amazing to see. He jumped through every obstacle and came running into my arms at the finish line. He beat his dad to the finish." Reflecting back on the event, Heidi says, "The most terrifying and important thing you can learn as a parent is when to let go, when to acknowledge it's safe to trust your kid. You have to have the courage to let them fly." Because both her husband and son completed the race, Heidi decided to do it, too, and she finished later that day.

How to Practice Making Fear Your Friend

Dr. Lara Pence

Almost every parent has experienced a child who is scared to death of something. The child's fear is so strong that it's paralyzing. My oldest son, Parker, had an extreme fear of going to the dentist. When he was just six years old, it was a nightmare. He would barely let a dentist look in his mouth, and he would shove away any tool that came close to going in. During a routine visit, the dentist noticed a cavity and recommended pulling the tooth. Parker's unwillingness to sit still would be a disaster for the procedure, so she suggested putting him under with anesthesia. *Oh my gosh*, I thought. *His fear of needles on top of his fear of the dentist will destroy him! How would he ever sit still while the anesthesiologist puts an IV in his arm?* When I told Parker what needed to happen, he sobbed. He obsessively asked questions: How big was the needle? Where would it go? Would they have to go inside his mouth? Would they use the scraper? I decided we needed a plan, an intervention. I'm a psychologist, for crying out loud!

So we went to work—together. We ended up

using several coping techniques that you can use, too. I decided we would also try a very useful tactic called "systematic desensitization," which sounds technical but is just repeated exposure to the fear-inducing situation, which leads to familiarity and significantly reduces the fear response. Here's how we practiced. Leading up to the procedure, we would stage "pretend visits" to the dentist. We would set up his bedroom as the dentist office. We would practice walking in, checking in with the office manager (played brilliantly by Parker's three-year-old brother), and sitting in the dentist chair. I worked with him on deep breathing techniques (we used the four-square method), and we would use mantras like "It's only my body getting scared; my smart mind knows it will be okay." I also pretended to be the dentist. I wore a mask, found a sewing needle, and asked him questions like the ones he would be asked so he would get used to the language.

We committed to this practice every night, and by the time his procedure rolled around, he was ready. In fact, he was a star. He didn't cry once, even when they had to stick him multiple times because they couldn't find a good vein. Parker actually laughed about it with the anesthesiologist. The dental team was stunned at his improvements and told me that they had never seen anything like it. But here's the thing: I knew he could do it. He just needed help, practice, and confidence.

As parents, we need to pay attention when fear is becoming paralyzing for our kids. This is a time when it's okay to step in and help out. We need to do a better job teaching our kids that feelings are just feelings—not facts—and that they have the capacity to manage their response. We can't control how we feel, but we can control our response to the feeling. We can't control being afraid, but we can control how we respond to fear. When we talk to our children, we need to let them know that fear will be an ever-present emotion in their lives, but it's not a bad emotion. It just signals that we may need to use certain skills to keep moving forward.

Teens: A Special Breed of Scaredy-Cat

Think your teenager is lazy? You may be mistaking laziness with *task avoidance*. Teens nowadays are especially vulnerable to worry and fear, and this can lead to avoidance. Here are some common fears that target teens:

1 *Fear of the spotlight (aka social anxiety).* Adolescents can become afraid of being the focus of attention, fearing that their flaws will be broadcast to their peers and beyond.
2 *Fear of failure.* Teens often avoid hard stuff because they want to avoid failing. Inadequate confidence and low self-esteem will lead them to retreat if failure is an option. They don't trust their abilities and would rather not try at all than try and fail.
3 *Fear of criticism.* Many teens are uncomfortable being judged, corrected, or scolded by authority

figures, so they avoid situations where that is possible. This is where the pursuit of perfection can rear its head—which is equally as destructive.

4 *Fear of rejection.* People-pleasing can become a real issue for some teens, especially the ones who are a little more type A, organized, perfectionistic, and naturally empathic. Some are so worried about rejection that they will hustle to please others at every moment.

5 *Competition comparison.* Some teens avoid sports or other challenges because they believe their performance will be compared to other kids'. Plus, for many kids, the misguided obsession of many *adults* with winning at all costs has sucked the fun out of playing sports.

How can you parent your teens through this? Well, you'll notice a common theme among all five fears: being judged. One of the best ways to help your children tolerate judgment is to remind them that there will always be critics. Tell them that life is like one big game. At any given moment, when they step out on the field, there will be people in the stands who will root for them and others who won't. That's okay. Not everyone has to be on our side in all circumstances. The key is deciding who you will choose to listen to—the rude, nasty fan who barks at you or the supportive, encouraging fan who cheers you on. You can't avoid judgment in life, but you can learn to shift focus.

In Conclusion

Fear can be either your friend or your foe. You can figure out how to use fear as fuel, or you can let it become just one more piece of bullshit that stands between your present self and who you want to be. I guess you could say that Spartan is in the fear business—we challenge people to meet their fear at the starting line and power through so it's gone by the finish line. Not surprisingly, I have found that Spartan is the first stop for many people who have another, bigger thing that they're afraid of—asking their girlfriend to marry them, leaving their cushy job and starting their own company, or signing up for that ultramarathon they've always wanted to do. If Spartan can be the gateway drug to greater courage for future challenges, I've done my job!

When it comes to your kids, don't forget that your fear does not need to become theirs. They have their own set of fears. The last thing they need is you telling them to be afraid of something new. Whether you're telling them with words or through actions, both are powerful agents of stagnation and timidity. Be bold, be brave, and be better.

Ready for Anything

Have Grit, Change the World

> Nobody owes you anything. If you can remember that, then you'll never take anything for granted.
>
> —Jerry Zaks, renowned performer, Broadway director, and son of Holocaust survivors

The youngest member of the 2020 Kids Death Race Team was Alex, one of my daughters. She was eight at the time, in a camp full of kids bigger than her. She endured eighteen consecutive hours of the Death Race. There's a moment we caught on camera that will stick with me forever. Alex was struggling, having trouble carrying rocks up the mountain, but she muscled through. The next day she came to me and said, "Yesterday, that little rock was heavy for me. Now, it's light."

And that's exactly what overcoming obstacles does for us: it alters our perception and makes us believe we can do hard things. Sometimes the littlest kids are the grittiest. This moment made me feel like I had come full circle, instilling a bit of the tough stuff my parents taught me in my own kids. Rocks have particular meaning for me as obstacles because they were part of my childhood, too.

As a kid, I worked for my father, doing some construction. My father came up to me one day and asked, "You see that big rock over there?"

"Yes."

"We have to move it. Can you move it?"

I looked at the rock, and it seemed like a massive boulder. There was no way I could move that rock. But I gave it a shot anyway.

I worked for an hour on that rock and couldn't move the thing.

I called my father and told him, "Hey, I can't move this boulder."

"No problem," he said. "I'll find someone who can."

That was all it took. I didn't want to be the guy who wasn't good enough. I didn't want to let someone else step in and do the job I couldn't do. I found a way to move that darn boulder.

My dad told me later that he knew all along that I could do it.

That moment has stuck with me for decades. I didn't know it at the time, but it was my dad's way of teaching me about perseverance and grit. From my dad to me. From me to my daughter. Generation to generation.

Our kids will have to move a lot of boulders in their lives. They'll have to solve huge problems that seem insurmountable, from the effects of pandemics and economic crises to the aftermath of climate disasters. The pandemic showed us how very unpredictable life can be. Sometimes school gets called off, and you have to cope. Sometimes bosses get sick, and you have to lead.

We can't know what's coming their way, but we can make sure our children have the strength and self-belief to keep going and persevere. We can make sure they practice handling adversity. That's how we can make them ready for anything.

Persistence is a powerful life skill. It's led me to where I am in life, and it is a character trait that guides many of the most successful people.

Take Kyle Dake, for instance. He's a four-time NCAA champion in four different weight classes, he's an Olympian, and he's been wrestling since he was four years old. Clearly, he's a physically talented guy, but a major part of his success is the way he thinks. Kyle is a die-hard optimist. And that came from wrestling. He doesn't think about losing but instead focuses on the next challenge. One thing he said that will always stick with me: "In your worst moment, you can find the good in it, no matter what." That's the essence of resilience.

When you're a wrestler, and you're stripped down to nothing but a thin singlet on an open mat, there's nothing to drive you forward other than your own positive thoughts, your own internal fire. Former Olympic wrestler Nate Carr once told me something that I now believe to be a critical truth for building grit: "Never personalize failure." When Nate lost a match, he didn't beat himself up afterward; instead, he analyzed his performance objectively. He thought, *My elbow position is the problem,* or, *I need to get lower to the ground.* In that way, all the responsibility for the loss still rested on his shoulders, but he had laid out concrete steps to take so he wouldn't fail again. That's grit in action.

We all need to look at our failures objectively and figure out what we need to do to succeed next time, and then try again. Too many of us wait until we're in the heart of our life to look at ourselves without judgment, to analyze and assess our skills without defensiveness or insecurity. But there's really no other way to build grit than to take an honest look at yourself so you can put in the hours, show up every day, and turn any failure into a success. Fail forward. We can all become self-made champions. This will build real grit.

True Grit

The majority of this book talks about true resilience. People often confuse the term *resilience* with another important term, *grit*. Resilience is really all about adversity; it's the ability to get through adverse situations—to consume failure for breakfast, challenge for lunch, and struggle for dinner. It's the attribute you call up when times get tough, you aren't sure if you can, and doing what's necessary isn't a well-paved path. Grit, on the other hand, is "perseverance and passion for long-term goals," according to psychologist Angela Duckworth.

Duckworth has studied grit for more than ten years and wrote the *New York Times* bestseller *Grit: The Power of Passion and Perseverance*. If grit is dogged tenaciousness, the obsession to reach a goal that is sustained for years, then resilience is like a primer for grit. Adversity is the price of resilience, and resilience is the price of grit.

Grit on the Outside Versus Grit on the Inside

Thanks to popular culture—the rough-and-tough cowboy, the pick-yourself-up-by-your-bootstraps tomboy, the stiff and rigid military figure—we often have an idea of what grit should look like. For many, the word *grit* conjures up images of Mattie Ross (Kim Darby) and Rooster Cogburn (John Wayne) in the classic 1969 western *True Grit*. And we often see grit celebrated on the silver screen through tough-as-nails actors like Sylvester Stallone, Clint Eastwood, and Brie Larson (Captain Marvel). The thing is, grit doesn't *look* any way at all. Grit happens internally, not externally.

I often come across people who try to impress me with their

toughness. They challenge me to see who can do more burpees in a minute, they curse incessantly, they throw stones at those who aren't quite as capable as they are, or they flash their warrior story in front of me. But the grittiest people I know, the ones who have that passion for the long-term game, are often quiet, subdued, and subtly confident. They have nothing to prove. They're so committed to the present steps that will take them to their future finish line that they don't have time to spew bullshit and play the part. They *are* the part.

Grit is an internal journey. Sure, celebrating your wins along the way, being proud of your accomplishments, and sharing your progress can help you reflect on the journey—where you've come from and how far you have to go—but true grit lies within. It's not a post on Instagram, a shirt that says FUCK OFF, or a virtue that you need to signal at every turn.

Kids often look for external rewards or evidence that signals certain characteristics. For example, they believe they are hardworking because teachers tell them so and they get good grades. They tell others they are kind because friends and family members have called them kind. They think of themselves as likable because they get invited to parties or have friends at school. Kids will often scan the external world for the internal validation of who they think they are. When it comes to grit, however, the small steps of perseverance and commitment matter, but sometimes there aren't any measurable steps to point to—just time. This can be hard for kids to understand because as they are building grit, they don't even know it.

Here's why talking about grit with your kids and naming that "I don't know why I feel good but I do" feeling is so important. If you can find small but significant steps that you can point out to your kids—awesome. But remember that grit comes in many forms and is sometimes invisible and internal.

Ready for Anything: For the Family

You can't teach your kids how to be persistent if you jump in and do everything for them at the first sign of difficulty or discomfort. But if you teach them to adopt a growth mindset, they will be moving through challenges with ease and determination before you know it.

You may recall that we discussed Carol Dweck, author of *Mindset: The New Psychology of Success*, in chapter 5. In her book, Dweck, now a professor of psychology at Stanford, distinguishes two types of people: those with a "fixed mindset," who believe that they are innately either good or bad at something, and those with a "growth mindset," who believe that they can change, learn from their mistakes, and eventually improve through practice.

In a landmark study in 1998, Dweck's research team gave fifth graders a test involving simple puzzles. After scoring the test, the researchers gave each student their grade and praised him or her randomly using one of two sentences. Some of the students were praised for their intelligence: "You must be smart at this." The others were praised for their effort: "You must have worked really hard."

Later, the students were offered a second test. They could choose another "easy" test like the first one, or they could select a harder one. All of the kids were told that they would learn a lot by trying the more challenging puzzles. The result? The majority of the kids who were praised for being smart chose the easy test, whereas 90 percent of the kids praised for their hard work and effort selected the harder one. Praising effort instead of intelligence fostered a growth mindset. And a growth mindset is the key to developing grit.

At her office at the University of Pennsylvania, Professor Duckworth talked to me at length about grit. She told me that grit predicts whether kids will be successful far more accurately than intelligence or a privileged upbringing. You may be wondering how you can make your kids gritty. Is grit about self-control, self-discipline, or the ability to delay gratification? I was surprised when Duckworth told me that grit and self-control, while related, are not the same thing. She pointed out that, although people who are good at overcoming temptation tend to be grittier, it's wrong to think high achievers have great self-control. She explained, "What's true of the most eminent individuals in society is that they have the capacity for zest and sustained hard labor."

For Duckworth, it's not self-control that makes gritty people so awesome. It's their ability to persevere and maintain hope in spite of setbacks and progress that never appears to arrive. But can grit be taught to kids? Yep. And here's how.

EIGHT WAYS TO DEVELOP GRITTY KIDS

1 *Look for passion, then be patient.* Duckworth argues that passion plus persistence equals grit. Grit evolves over time. But passion comes first, before perseverance, she says. "And it has nothing to do with parents chaining their kids to the violin stand."

If kids find something that interests them, they'll be much more inclined to develop persistence and grit naturally on their own.

Duckworth says it's important at early ages for kids to explore and develop interests. "There's a developmental progression," she explains. "If you look at graphs of grit by age, you see it's not realistic to think that kids at seven, eight, fourteen, or sixteen will have a goal that they will pursue with all of their heart for decades at all costs and do hours of deliberate practice a day and be incredibly resilient."

So allow your children to go out for the soccer team, try learning the guitar, join a Scout troop, take a martial arts class. Expose your kids to many different activities and skill-building opportunities. Help your children see for themselves that the way to grow as a human being is to take on new and interesting challenges. Channel their energy toward opportunities that are meaningful. Eventually, something will stick. The seeds of passion will be planted and will begin to grow along with maturity. With maturity, perseverance and persistence for their passions will emerge, and grit will be born.

2 **Focus on the effort, not the result.** Remember Dweck's research? Praise the effort—"Wow, you're working very hard on this"—rather than the result. It still shows your enthusiasm for what they've done without implying that your acceptance depends on the score of the game or how well they performed. Celebrate the process, not just the product. When

your kid comes home with a C on a paper even though they worked hard, it's okay to let them know that you expect better next time and then also highlight how hard they worked, the effort they put in, and what they learned in the process. This part is essential for later on in life because, as we know, life doesn't always go our way. The more practice they have in appreciating the process, the less likely they will be to crumble when a future end result doesn't work out in their favor. If you praise grittiness and determination, your children will learn to value those traits, rather than obsess about short-term results.

3 *Build on failure.* Resilience and grit are built on a foundation of failure. Struggle and mistakes are part of life, and if your kids don't have the opportunity to fail, they'll never learn that they can bounce back. Convince your kids that failing is the surest path to long-term success. Make it clear that it's okay to fail as long as they learn lessons from the failure and continue forward toward their goals. They simply can't build grit if everything is too easy. I know this is an overplayed example, but they've got to get back on the horse when they fall, or the bike, for that matter—choose your mode of transportation! The "try again" method is essential for building on failure. Even if they fall off again, you're teaching them the power of recovery and persistence. It's that "fail forward" mentality that will allow them to have incredible perspective throughout life.

4 *Add stress in small doses.* We've demonized stress in our culture, but children need stress in their lives

so that they can learn how to cope with it. One of the world's most renowned experts on resilience, Michael Rutter of King's College London, is famous for his landmark studies of Romanian orphans. His work demonstrated that children's interaction with their environment matters as much to their growth and development as their temperament, IQ, or genes. Just as early exposure to a germ can inoculate a child against infection later on, exposure to external stress offers a "steeling effect" that builds resilience. Rutter says that resilience is more than a personality trait; it's a process. What kind of stress is good for your kids? Encourage them to try something new—a new food, sport, playground, tree to climb, math puzzle. Find something unfamiliar every week.

5   *Discourage easy outs.* Grit comes from the daily discipline of trying to do things better today than we did yesterday. So don't let your kids quit an activity or sport when it gets hard or else they'll have a difficult time developing grit. "Getting back on the [horse] the next day, eager to try again, is in my view even more reflective of grit," Duckworth writes in *Grit*. "When you don't come back the next day—when you permanently turn your back on a commitment—your effort plummets to zero. As a consequence, your skills stop improving, and at the same time, you stop producing anything with whatever skills you already have."

6   *Encourage kids to step outside the box.* Admittedly, this isn't the easiest thing to teach a kid—or

an adult, for that matter. Like a stream of water, we humans naturally seek the path of least resistance. But that's no way to develop grit. To get grit, we need to regularly face and defeat mental and physical obstacles. This is something you can teach your kids by putting them into situations of "deliberate adversity" and encouraging them to step outside their own comfort box. It can be scary at first, but soon your kids will *know* that they can handle anything. Try these "hard way" activities for starters:

- Sign them up for an obstacle course race.
- Make them do an activity with other kids they don't know.
- Send them away to an overnight camp for a week.
- Require them to do a different sport every season.
- Challenge them to introduce themselves to a peer who intimidates and interests them.
- Encourage them to ask the coach if they can play a new position on their team.
- Have them deal with a problem at school without your involvement.

These situations will test their strength, sharpen their ability to deal with surprises and setbacks, and ultimately teach them what they're made of.

7 *Teach optimism.* The Spartans practiced optimism from a young age by deliberately experiencing adversity. According to Plutarch, the Greek biogra-

pher who wrote the definitive history of Sparta, the Spartans intentionally slept on hard pallets, wore no shoes, owned one piece of clothing, and followed a near-starvation diet. Why? Because they knew that when people get used to life in the tough lane, they are better able to handle challenging surprises and to adjust their approach accordingly. Those who have learned how to overcome obstacles tend to have a positive outlook under even the harshest conditions.

Use language with your children that fosters hope and optimism. Teach them that a positive outlook helps breed confidence and interest in pushing forward. Correct them when they say things like "It will never go my way" or "I'll always be bad at this." Remind them that words like *never* and *always* have no place in your family unless they are attached to something hopeful. And share with them stories of your own optimism and hope. Introduce them to characters and real-life people who have persevered. Who's more inspiring—a *Fortnite* character or Mulan, Martin Luther King Jr., and Muhammad Ali?

8 **Teach them to be 100 percent responsible for their outcomes.** I didn't grow up wrestling, but I'm a big fan of the sport. Why? Well, I've traveled the world talking to highly successful people—entrepreneurs, yogis, athletes, professors, actors, and military personnel—and I noticed something strange: a disproportionate number of highly effective people grew up wrestling.

I started to realize that there's something about

wrestling that teaches you to become resilient and persevering, the key traits of an entrepreneur. In any wrestling match, you only have two things to work with: your body and your training. That puts 100 percent of the responsibility for success or failure on you. Either you're not strong enough or you're not using the right technique. You can't blame others. You can't make excuses.

Kids need to learn that when they make certain choices, those choices have outcomes—sometimes it's a good outcome; other times, not so much. It's easy as a parent to swoop in and say that it wasn't their fault or that sometimes bad stuff just happens. It's a lot more difficult to tolerate their sadness or disappointment by acknowledging that they had a hand in the final poor outcome. Here's where you have to think about the future. If you parent your kids now to understand responsibility, they will carry this with them into adulthood. We all know some annoying adults who never take responsibility for anything. Don't let your kid become that adult— start teaching your children responsibility now.

Throughout this book, I've outlined the path to true resilience for you and your family, and I've highlighted the biggest missteps you're likely to make on that journey. All of us fall short of our ideals sometimes, especially when it comes to our families. But if we let go of perfection and let ourselves roll with the wonders and difficulties of life with kids, we're going to be more joyful and adaptive parents. So let's reframe the "don'ts" as "dos." Let's ask ourselves how we can turn our leadership patterns into actionable opportunities for growth and joy. Get out a pen and ask yourself these questions. Jot down your first response to each. If you have more than one child, you may have more than one answer to each question.

1 What am I doing for my kids that they could do for themselves?
2 When my children are experiencing a difficult emotion, how can I take a step back and let them work through those feelings?
3 What should I say no to the next time my kids push for it?
4 What do I want my kids to see me doing?
5 What one rule do I want to enforce on a daily basis?
6 What is one mature behavior I can demand from my children?
7 What fears (from ticks to a fear of heights) am I discussing in front of my children, and how can I talk about it in a way that is productive?
8 What would be an exciting and slightly scary challenge for my kids?
9 What outdoor game or activity would be fun to play with my children?
10 What natural wonder would I like to take my kids to experience?
11 What must my children accomplish before they get screen time?
12 What is something that I'm good at that I've always wanted to teach my children?

You may not have an answer for all of these questions, but I do hope they inspire you to think about how you want your family to live. The point is to find your own style within a framework of firmness, accountability, and confidence. Overparenting often robs us of our creativity, spontaneity, and intentionality as parents. When we are trying to fill every minute of the day with activities, "keep up with the Joneses," and do everything "perfectly," we miss moments to share adventures with our kids. If you embrace imperfection and plan a little less, you'll wind up doing more for your children.

In Conclusion

Grit is built through commitment, perseverance, and sticking to it when things get hard. Your kids deserve to be challenged in a way that doesn't provide immediate reward and reinforcement. You can push them toward anything worthwhile to support the building of grit: music, swimming, math, science, chemistry, language, wrestling, dance, running, art—whatever is meaningful to you and them. By pushing your children to train harder in judo or practice the piano longer—even if they are resistant—you'll help them build skill and resilience through failure and struggle, and then you can watch them enjoy and benefit from their hard work. The result is that they will perform well in that discipline, which feeds their passion and sets them up for a successful life.

It can be rough when reality hits, and the world is getting more complicated and competitive by the minute. Our nation, and our planet, needs a rising generation of survivors who can call on their problem-solving skills, resilience, and flexibility like their own emotional Swiss Army knife. Yes, kids can handle extreme stress and be better for it. Yes, kids can work hard to bring about progress and innovation and health. I believe the number one gift we have no choice but to force upon our kids is fluency in overcoming obstacles. That skill correlates with their success.

A snowy mountain can and will be climbed. A Montauk swim can and will be finished. A global pandemic can and will be overcome. No one will hand out medals for these things. But depth of character, endurance, and resilience will be trained, ingrained, and passed down for generations.

My mom and dad said the same thing before they died. With your kids, they said, you will often have to choose either the hard way or the easy way. Almost always choose the hard way. You will end up with better adults.

Let's do this. Let's raise resilient kids who are ready for anything.

Conclusion

As Dr. L and I were putting the finishing touches on this book, she reached out to my wife to ensure that Courtney felt good about the product that we had developed. My family and I were in Jackson Hole, Wyoming, just starting our spring break ski trip with the kids. She caught Courtney early on a Saturday morning as she was getting ready to head down to the airport to pick up our son Jack, who was just fifteen. He was flying across the country from Boston to Wyoming all by himself, possibly without a charged phone. "He'll be fine," Courtney told Dr. L. "You know, it's one of those moments where you hope your child knows what he's doing, but if he misses his flight, he'll figure out a way to let us know or get here somehow." Dr. L mentioned to me later that it was refreshing to catch my wife and me in a moment of truly walking the walk—letting our kid solve problems on his own, build confidence, and navigate the world without constant supervision and attention.

I've realized through the years of building a global brand and navigating the trials of parenthood that many people believe that compartmentalization is the key to success. Believe me, I've tried this route. When my parents got divorced, I learned to compartmentalize. As the stress of their volatile marriage came to an end, it was more data that told me we have to be able to turn off the tough shit—separate home life from outside life—when necessary. Things that were stressful and scary had to be put away or dealt with quickly so we could move on. Many say that this is a strength of mine today—that when shit gets tough, I take the approach of FFIO (fucking figure it out) rather than sitting and stewing and dwelling. But here's a secret: life is actually *more* fulfilling when we learn to integrate instead of compartmentalize. The truth is that our family life bleeds into our work life, and our work life bleeds into our family life. Why? Because as adults, how we show up to do anything is how we show up to do everything. You may *think* you're good at separating these facets of your life, but I promise they'll catch up with you somewhere.

I learned this the hard way when I suffered a stroke after traveling the world during my first book tour, as we were opening up Spartan races in Asia. That week, I had spent more hours flying than I had sleeping, and pushing my body to the brink left me wildly dehydrated. As a result, a clot jumped from one side of my heart to the other and clogged a tiny vein controlling my eyesight. I woke up one morning and literally couldn't see. I spent thirty days in the hospital—still taking cold showers and doing burpees in the stairwell, of course. I was forced to take a look at what was sustainable and decide how I wanted to show up as a dad because it was possible that if I didn't change things, I wouldn't be able to show up at all. You may think that I slowed down, chilled out, and learned to stop and smell the roses. Not really. But I did learn that no time on this planet is guaranteed and that if I want to make my mark as a business owner and as a father, then I have to be more intentional, more focused.

If there's any lesson that I want you to take from this book, it's just that: be more intentional, more focused—as a human and as a parent. I know all the excuses about why you can't. You're too tired, too overwhelmed, too stressed, too this, too that. And sure, some would argue that parents are more focused now than they've ever been. But as I've highlighted in these pages, we aren't dialing in to the *right* things. We're prioritizing abundance over adversity, success over struggle, perfection over purpose, and fun over failure. As a result, we are lonelier than we've ever been, more disconnected, and less healthy, and our kids are running right along beside us, feeling the same way. Choosing the harder route is not alluring. I get it. But I believe that many of us feel the ground underneath sinking. We are craving more, and we want better.

If we learn to focus on what really matters and be more intentional with our own choices, we can parent from this same position. As you start to recognize your own excuses, you'll parent with less tolerance for your kid's excuses. As you become more consistent with your routine, you'll enforce a routine for your children. As you begin to accept your own failures, you'll become willing to let your kids fail. Discipline will breed discipline. Courage will beget courage. Cultivation of true resilience in you will grow resilience in your kids. It will eventually all fall into line, and you will notice changes.

Patience, consistency, and willingness are all required to move forward. And you've got everything you need to start today. Know that I am doing the work, too—every single day. When Jack can't look up from his iPhone, Charlie wants to skip wrestling, Catherine rolls her eyes at Courtney, and Alex can't help but reach for the candy bars at checkout, I too am taking the more difficult route of reeling that back in and parenting with resilience in mind. We all have to participate in this enormous challenge together and make a commitment to parent better. I know there's a saying out there: *when they go low, we go high.* Let's start a new one: when they go easy, we go hard. I'm in. Are you?

Acknowledgments

FROM JOE

Like putting together a Spartan race, writing a book takes a village. I'd like to thank the following people, without whom this book would have just remained an idea in my head.

First, to the Spartan community whose stories of courage and commitment are an endless well of inspiration: I never imagined that when I started this journey that all who flocked to the starting line would provide a constant stream of reasons for me to get after it and keep pushing limits. Thank you for showing up and living every day like a true Spartan.

Next, to my team at Spartan: I am lucky to be surrounded by some of the most enthusiastic and energized people on this planet. Jeff Connor, Jeff Gerlach, David Piperno, Mike Morris, David Watson, Donny Jensen, Jon Oustaev, Kyle McLaughlin, Erin Sutton, and the whole team at both Spartan and Tough Mudder—you guys are fucking amazing. Each and every day you pour your heart into our mission and I am so thankful that I've got the best pit crew on the planet. A special thanks to Kristen Dollard for her attention to this project. And to Susan Kelley, who helps keep the whole ship afloat.

To the team at HarperCollins, you all cleaned the muck and grime off of my vision and gave it clarity. Thank you for the amazing support and encouragement.

Now, to my extended family and friends: To my grandparents, aunts, and uncles, who have supported me constantly, even when I had the craziest ideas. To my sister, T, who shares so much of our mother's amazing spirit and passion for life and is always there for me and our family. To Ian, Sarah, Heather, and Liam Lawson—thanks for years of love and support. To Al Capucci, who put up guardrails when I needed them. To the mob bosses, who schooled me back in Queens, and to my childhood friends, who helped me build the first obstacle race ever—the BMX track.

To the Jain family, who are the best kind of friends to have and explore the world with. Bobby and Carola are always my go-to people for grounded, loyal, and trusted advice. And to the Borden family, who makes Vermont not more than tolerable but fucking awesome.

To Courtney's parents, Bob and Laurel, who have supported our family since day one. They have traveled the world to be with us and are always up for anything. As Courtney mentioned, they make the small things matter, whether it's through family dinners or practicing spelling words. After fifty-three years of marriage they are an incredible example of teamwork, unconditional love, marriage, and what it is to be a loving parent. I feel grateful to have them in our lives.

To my dad, who taught me that it could always be worse and to take the lessons where and when you could. To my mom, who was truly the first modern-day Spartan and is a never-ending source of motivation.

And last but never least, to my family: To my kids, Jack, Charlie, Catherine, and Alex, who challenge me just as much as I challenge them. This book would not be possible without the stories, the trials, and the laughs that we have created as a family. And finally, to my incredible wife, Courtney, who reminds me that love must be front and center and puts up with my wild antics at every turn. She is hands down my favorite parent out there.

FROM DR. L

To my clients, past and present, kids and adults and parents. My work as a psychologist is shaped substantially by each of you. For the past twenty years, you have trusted me with your stories and given me a special permission slip to see the most vulnerable and scary parts of your world. Any client that steps into the office after you benefits because of you. Our work together is etched into the fiber of who I am and who I will be. Thank you.

To the team at HarperCollins—Sydney, Dan, Julia, and every other brilliant soul: your unwavering support, enthusiasm, and guidance has made this come to life. Thank you for seeing how necessary this book is and for believing in it from the start.

To my family: I'll start first with the Edmunds. Thank you to the entire family for embracing me from day one and weaving me into the fold of your family in the most beautiful way. Specifically, Papa E. and Granny—I am perhaps the luckiest person on the planet to have landed an additional set of parents who are just as loving and extraordinary as my own. Thank you.

To my sister, thank you for both the silliness and the challenge. It's a wild blend but we make it work.

To my dad, you taught me to make magic. You showed me how to believe in the emotion of the experience not just in what you see. From *David Copperfield* to *Brigadoon*, it all comes down to the feeling you create and the hard work that lies underneath. Thank you.

To my mom, this entire book—the lessons, the words, the knowledge, the commitment to the work—it all comes from you. Your resilience is abundant. Your courage is extraordinary. Your discipline is unparalleled. Every day you show me what a human being is really capable of. Thank you.

To Parker and Keaton, thank you both for making this parenting journey so riveting. You keep me on my toes and make it fun. You both embody the spirit of this book, and I love you to pieces.

To Carey, my preferred person in all endeavors. You are the best thing that I have ever worked hard for.

About the Authors

JOE DE SENA is the CEO and founder of the world's leading endurance sports and extreme wellness brand Spartan. He is also the *New York Times* bestselling author of *Spartan Up!* and *Spartan Fit!*, and an accomplished adventure racer. He is the host of the *Spartan Up!* podcast and lives in Vermont with his wife and their four children.

DR. LARA PENCE, PsyD, MBA, is a licensed clinical psychologist who has helped hundreds of individuals and their families go from unhealthy and stuck to healthy and resilient. She is the founder of LIGHFBOX and the official Spartan Mind Doc. She lives in Colorado with her husband and their two children.